EMOTIONAL HEALING
MADE SIMPLE

*Tricia,
Merry Christmas 2023-24
and
Happy New Year
I love you forever!
♡ DeeDee
xo*

EMOTIONAL HEALING
MADE SIMPLE

Praying Medic

INKITY
PRESS™

© Copyright 2023 – Praying Medic

All rights reserved. This book is protected by the copyright laws of the United States of America. No portion of this book may be stored electronically, transmitted, copied, reproduced or reprinted for commercial gain or profit without prior written permission from Inkity Press™. Permission requests may be emailed to **admin@inkitypress.com** or sent to the Inkity Press mailing address below. Only the use of short quotations or occasional page copying for personal or group study is allowed without written permission.

Unless otherwise noted, all scripture quotations are taken from the New King James Version®. Copyright © 1982 by Thomas Nelson, Inc. Used by permission. All rights reserved.

Inkity Press™
137 East Elliot Road, #2292, Gilbert, AZ 85299

This book and other Inkity Press titles can be found at:
PrayingMedic.com

Available at Amazon.com and other retail outlets.

For more information visit our website at **www.inkitypress.com**
or email us at **admin@inkitypress.com** or **admin@prayingmedic.com**

ISBN-13: 978-1-947968-10-3 (Inkity Press)

Printed in the U.S.A.

DEDICATION

TO THOSE WHO HAVE OVERCOME the horrors of trauma-based mind control. Each of you is a testimony to the healing power of God's love.

TABLE OF CONTENTS

Introduction 9
Chapter 1   I Don't Think I Need Emotional Healing 13
2   How the Soul Is Wounded and How It Is Healed 17
3   Childhood Trauma 21
4   The Development of Alternate Personalities 25
5   My Emotional Healing 31
6   A Simple Approach to Emotional Healing 35
7   Emotional Healing: The Long Path 39
8   Overnight Healing 41
9   Yelena's Healing 43
10   Are You Ready To Be Healed? 47
11   A Firefighter Healed of PTSD 51
12   A Healing Dialogue with God 55
13   Removing Evil Spirits 59
14   Emotional Healing of Back Pain 73
15   Emotional Roots of Physical Illness 79
16   Healed of Alcoholism 83
17   Healing Through Worship 85
18   The Spiritual Senses 87
19   The Other Me 93
20   Interacting in the Spirit 97
21   Jesus Heals and Integrates an Alter 103
22   Anita's Healing and Deliverance 109
23   Diana Jamerson's Testimony 113
24   Angels Help with Deliverance 117
25   The Spectrum of Mind Control 119
26   Svali – A Former Illuminati Trainer 123
➤➤➤   **Important Warning: Sensitive Content 125**
27   Trauma-Based Mind Control: Terminology 127
28   Methods of Illuminati Programming 131
29   Programming Themes and Internal Structures 143
30   Brain Wave Programming 153
31   Near Death, Assassin, and CIA Programming 157
32   Types of Alters and Fragments 165
33   Healing the Survivor 171
34   Learning to Love 177

NOTE

The subject of this book is the healing of emotional trauma. Traditionally, this issue is addressed from two distinct perspectives. It falls under the purview of those who practice professionally in the field of mental health, but it is also treated by non-clinicians. My approach to this subject is purely from a non-clinical perspective. I am not qualified to diagnose mental health disorders, and I am not a licensed therapist or counselor. If you feel you need a diagnosis, or if you desire therapy or counseling, please seek help from a qualified, licensed mental health professional. The information presented in this book is not intended to be a substitute for the expertise and treatment offered by mental health professionals.

INTRODUCTION

THREE YEARS AFTER GRADUATING FROM high school, at the urging of my mother, I enrolled in a class that would train me to become an emergency medical technician. Over the next 35 years, I responded to calls that exposed me to emotional trauma almost daily. On August 8, 2008, I had a life-changing encounter with God, who instructed me to pray for my patients and assured me He would heal them.

In 2009, I began seeing a few people healed of physical injuries and illnesses. I wrote about those stories on a website. A year later, I began discussing supernatural healing on Facebook and became friends with thousands of people around the world who were operating in healing and deliverance. What I learned in these early years would become the foundation for my first book, *Divine Healing Made Simple*.

In 2011, I moved to Arizona and took a job where I often transported people from hospital emergency departments to mental health treatment centers. After seeing my patients healed of physical ailments, I wondered if God could heal conditions like post-traumatic stress disorder, depression, and schizophrenia. A couple of friends were experiencing success with emotional healing, and they shared their observations with me. One friend, Matt Evans, was kind enough to help me with the healing of my own emotional trauma. (I'll share that story shortly.)

For the next few years, I studied the various approaches to emotional healing that had been developed by Christian ministries. The problem for me was that most of the methods used at the time required a minimum of two hours to complete. My job as a paramedic allowed me an average of fifteen minutes with a patient. I needed a process that was quick and effective.

In reviewing the various approaches to emotional healing, I noticed that nearly everyone used a couple of principles. I wondered if I stripped away everything else and focused on these key concepts if I could get people healed of emotional trauma. The theory proved to be valid. I developed a short, effective model for emotional healing that I've used successfully with thousands of people since then. The steps are outlined in my book, *Emotional Healing in 3 Easy Steps.*

Emotional trauma occurs on a spectrum from minor to severe. Minor trauma can be healed through relatively simple steps, but more severe trauma requires a different process. This book will explore the full spectrum of trauma—from minor to severe—and how it can be healed. First, we'll explore the causes of minor trauma and how it can be healed. Then, we'll examine the ways in which severe emotional trauma is inflicted, and how it is healed. (Trigger warnings are provided at the beginning of chapters that contain graphic descriptions of abuse.)

While the Bible has much to say about removing demons, it has little to say about healing emotional trauma. Many people are surprised to learn that the two are inextricably connected. I'll provide the scriptural foundation that describes how demons are removed. And I'll offer a biblical explanation of how emotional trauma occurs and why it can be healed. As it turns out, that discussion is more theoretical than practical. There are few accounts in the Bible describing the process of emotional healing. Therefore, testimonies will be used as illustrations to teach the principles that must be learned. These principles can also be conveyed through storytelling. Healing severe emotional trauma is the subject of my first novel, *The Gates of Shiloh.* The process described in that book through allegory will be explored in this book through the testimonies of people who have been healed.

~ Praying Medic

CHAPTER ONE

I Don't Think I Need Emotional Healing

SOME FIND THE IDEA OF emotional healing frightening. Others find it irrelevant. Objections to emotional healing and concerns about its practice are usually based on misunderstandings of what it is and what it is not.

For several years in the past, my wife, Denise, attended secular counseling sessions with a licensed therapist. While some people have received great benefits from counseling, she did not. Her sessions consisted of rehashing negative events from her past, crying over them, and never finding resolution. To her, counseling seemed pointless. I don't wish to paint all types of counseling with a broad brush. I realize that counseling can take many forms and that some people benefit from it.

Some believe that emotional healing is equivalent to counseling. And if they've had a negative experience with counseling, they may feel emotional healing isn't worth exploring. Emotional healing does have one feature in common with counseling therapy. In both practices, events from the past are recalled. In therapy, emotions are explored; but in emotional healing, God removes negative feelings altogether. In many cases, once a negative emotion related to a past event has been healed, that event need not be brought up again. If you're afraid that exploring your past may be too painful, I can assure you that if you're willing to recall a painful experience once, there's usually no need to do it again. On the rare occasion when a painful event is discussed more than once, it is usually because multiple negative emotions are associated with it. Once all the negative emotions related to an event are healed, the event can be forgotten. And if it does come to mind in the future, the pain that was previously associated with it will be absent.

Some think they do not need emotional healing because they believe that time heals all wounds. The truth is that time does not heal emotional wounds. It may actually worsen the effect of emotional wounds that remain unhealed.

Some think they do not need emotional healing because they easily forgive others and don't hold grudges. It is healthy to forgive others and refrain from harboring resentment. However, emotional healing has little to do with holding grudges or forgiveness. It's about healing the trauma inflicted on our souls by unexpected events and the people with whom we interact. Some of the most forgiving people in the world are deeply wounded by emotional trauma.

Some think they do not need emotional healing because they believe the difficulties they've endured have made them a better person. Life's difficulties may make one stronger, but they create emotional wounds that leave one vulnerable to sickness and demonic harassment.

Some believe they've never suffered emotional trauma. Being bullied by an older brother or sister can cause emotional trauma. So can being embarrassed by a teacher, ridiculed by a parent, or dumped by a lover. The death of a close friend or family member, the loss of a job, a divorce, or being the victim of online harassment can cause emotional trauma. I don't know anyone who has managed to escape emotional wounds through the course of their life.

I Don't Think I Need Emotional Healing

As you read the following chapters, you will likely become aware of how your soul has been traumatized. When you do, take heart. You'll also discover the ways in which it can be healed. The following testimony was submitted by a woman named Rachel, who did not think she needed emotional healing.

> Hi Dave. After learning about your emotional healing technique through your Telegram channel and videos, I began to invite God to speak to me about emotional wounds that might be at the root of some of the chronic illness I was experiencing. I think it was that very night that I had a dream where I was telling a woman how hurt I was when a little boy I had cared for from the time he was 18 months to around age six had moved out of state. I woke up with tears running down my face.
>
> I went through the steps and felt the emotional burden of that pain lift off of me. If I had been asked prior to that dream whether I had an emotional wound tied to that loss, I would have said no. Because my personality leans towards logical processing, the emotions just got boxed up and put into storage without much awareness on my part. But my Father, in His wisdom, saw the wound and offered healing. He's done that several times since with wounds or worries that aren't really registering in my waking mind. He draws them into my awareness, almost always through a dream, and invites me into a greater measure of the healing that Jesus won for all of God's family.

CHAPTER TWO

How the Soul is Wounded and How It Is Healed

AT CONCEPTION, GOD PLACES A spirit from heaven inside a fertilized egg, and a soul is formed. When the soul is created, it is crafted in perfection. It is unblemished, and in a sense, it is like a clean slate—waiting to be written upon by the world. Every interaction with another spirit or soul leaves an impression on us. Our soul is shaped by the interactions we have. Every video we watch, each interaction we have with a coworker, all our demonic dreams, and every encounter with God impacts the person we are becoming. Positive influences cause our souls to prosper. Negative influences inflict damage. The cumulative impacts and effects upon our soul over a lifetime mold and shape us into whom and what we are, for better or worse.

The person we are today is largely a product of our experiences—that, and the DNA from which we were created. The soul has the capacity of free choice. The ability of the soul to direct itself cannot be overridden by any living being without the soul's consent, and the will of God does not negate its choices. The soul can choose whether to love or to hate, to curse or bless, and to accept or reject all things in creation. The will of the soul—and the choices it makes—form the personality of an individual. The capacity to develop a unique personality based on collective choices and experiences is what the soul does. It creates the personality.

To explain the mechanism of emotional trauma, I'd like to illustrate how physical trauma damages the physical human body. When the body suffers physical trauma, several actions occur. If, for example, the trauma is a knife wound, the blood vessels damaged by the knife edge will bleed. Sensory nerves send electrical impulses to the brain that are interpreted as pain. If the wound is not cleaned, other living beings, such as bacteria, can inhabit the wound, and it may become infected. If the infection spreads, it may cause sepsis and affect the entire body. Physical trauma can be healed with the use of a cleansing agent, antibiotics, and proper wound care.

Similarly, the soul can be wounded by trauma. Since the soul is the place where emotions are processed, the trauma suffered by the soul is not physical, but emotional. Just as physical trauma can involve burns, electrical shock, and blunt trauma, the soul can be wounded in various ways. Verbal abuse is perhaps the most common cause of emotional trauma. Physical and sexual abuse and abandonment all cause emotional wounds as well.

Emotional trauma changes us in at least two distinct ways. First, it affects the way in which we interact with others. If one has had traumatic experiences with law enforcement officers, for example, they are likely to be distrustful of the police. If one has been abused by their father, they may resist the claim that God the Father can be trusted. Emotional trauma also changes us physically.

In the same way that bacteria can inhabit a physical wound if it is not properly cared for, evil spirits can inhabit soul wounds. Just as bacterial infection can cause sickness affecting the entire body, demons can cause ailments that affect the physical body. Many diseases and chronic pain syndromes are manifestations of demons that are attached to emotional wounds of the soul. The degree to which the soul and body are affected is determined by the severity of emotional trauma and the particular type of demons involved.

If we have physical or emotional problems presently, they may be the result of events that happened in our past. If we want to change our present behavior and if we're going to live in good physical health, we must change the way emotional trauma from the past affects us.

The healing of emotional trauma is poorly understood among believers, perhaps because it is not clearly demonstrated in the Bible. You can read through the New Testament gospels and find demonstrations of physical healing, miracles, and deliverance from evil spirits, but that is not so for emotional healing. However, the Bible does address the subject.

The book of Isaiah revealed much about the ministry of the Messiah hundreds of years in advance. Consider the following passage where Jesus taught in the synagogue:

So He came to Nazareth, where He had been brought up. And as His custom was, He went into the synagogue on the Sabbath day, and stood up to read. And He was handed the book of the prophet Isaiah. And when He had opened the book, He found the place where it was written:

"The Spirit of the Lord is upon Me,
Because He has anointed Me
To preach the gospel to the poor;
He has sent Me to heal the brokenhearted,
To proclaim liberty to the captives
And recovery of sight to the blind,
To set at liberty those who are oppressed;
To proclaim the acceptable year of the Lord."

Then He closed the book, and gave it back to the attendant and sat down. And the eyes of all who were in the synagogue were fixed on Him. And He began to say to them, "Today this Scripture is fulfilled in your hearing."
LK. 4:16-21

Jesus fulfilled the long-awaited prophecy of the Messiah. One segment of the prophecy says: "He has sent Me to heal the brokenhearted." The Hebrew word for brokenhearted, "sabar" (Strong's #H7665), means to break in pieces. Jesus came to heal anyone whose heart (or soul) had been shattered into pieces. How is a soul shattered into pieces? Emotional trauma causes wounds to the soul. The parts of a wounded soul are the broken or shattered pieces referenced in this verse. Jesus puts the broken parts of the soul back together through the process of healing and integration. (Later chapters will cover in greater detail how these parts of the soul are created and how they are healed.)

Now, consider this prophecy about the Messiah:

> *He is despised and rejected by men,*
> *A Man of sorrows and acquainted with grief.*
> *And we hid, as it were, our faces from Him;*
> *He was despised, and we did not esteem Him.*
> *Surely He has borne our griefs*
> *And carried our sorrows;*
> *Yet we esteemed Him stricken,*
> *Smitten by God, and afflicted.*
> *But He was wounded for our transgressions,*
> *He was bruised for our iniquities;*
> *The chastisement for our peace was upon Him,*
> *And by His stripes we are healed.*
> ISA. 53:3-5

In this passage, a prophecy is given that the torture of the Messiah (Jesus) would provide a way for us to be healed. This idea is usually applied to physical healing, but the prophet indicated that it applied to emotional healing as well. He wrote: "Surely He has borne our griefs and carried our sorrows." Grief and sorrow are painful emotions caused by trauma. If Jesus has borne these negative emotions for us, we no longer need to bear them. We can literally give our negative emotions to Him. The chapters that follow will explain this process in more detail.

CHAPTER THREE

Childhood Trauma

THE WAY IN WHICH WE respond to present conflicts was shaped in our souls during our youth. When we faced traumatic events and challenges as a child, we developed ways of responding to them—sometimes developing appropriate responses and sometimes not.

When we accept Jesus as our savior, the Spirit of God takes up residence in us; His Spirit provides insights and perspective (illumination) of the events we experience. If Jesus was not a part of our life when we were three years old, we learned to respond to the events of life without the light of God to guide us. Although we may have the light of God in us today, if our patterns of behavior were developed before that light was present, we will respond in ways that were developed in relative darkness. In our youth, we learn to respond to a specific event with an emotion. If we react with joy to a certain event, memories of that event and the attached emotions are made. If we respond with fear to an event, it leaves a memory in our soul, reminding us that we reacted with fear. Later in life, we may face a similar event. If we recall the memory of the previous event and how we reacted, it may cause us to react the same way. This leaves another memory of a fear response. The new memory increases the likelihood that we'll respond with fear to a similar future event. Later still, the response of fear can become generalized to all similar events. Each event leaves its own memories that further reinforce the same response. The soul's ability to be trained to respond in predictable ways is not unlike the way a computer can be programmed to perform specific tasks when certain conditions are met. When we experience sudden rage, it's often because the memory of an event from our past is being triggered. When we feel rejection, self-doubt, hopelessness, or any other negative emotion, there is usually the memory of an event from our past being triggered.

When we reflect on a painful event, we may see the event in our mind and feel the pain associated with it all over again. This is because the nature of the soul is both intellectual and emotional. The fabric of the soul is a canvas of thoughts and feelings.

One of my most vivid childhood memories was watching my two younger brothers cry hysterically as my mother cut their hair against their wishes. We were young teenagers, and it was the 1970s. Wearing long hair was a sign that you were cool. We'd reached the age where we no longer wanted the childish haircuts my mother gave us. Our older brothers had gone through the adult rites of passage and wore their hair as long as they wanted. We had not yet arrived. I was next for a haircut, and like my brothers, this particular one was emotionally traumatic for me. To this present moment, the memory of my mother cutting my hair that day still surfaces from time to time. I did not realize then that the memory and the emotions of anger I felt toward her would cause problems decades later.

Children (even teenagers) don't have the capacity to reason that adults have. Events that seem harmless to an adult can be terrifying to a child. As adults, we can view things through the lens of maturity and life experience. If we believe there isn't any actual harm in something that causes a child to be fearful, we will rationalize away the terrors they express. To us, their fears may seem foolish. Small children have a limited capacity to cope with strong emotions. A three-year-old who is lost for five minutes in a crowded grocery store can become so overwhelmed with anxiety and fear that their soul is deeply wounded. A child who is accidentally locked in a dark room alone for ten minutes before an adult finds them can suffer serious emotional trauma. To the child gripped with fear, anger, or some other negative emotion, the horror they feel is real, and it has an enduring effect. Events that seem harmless to an adult can cause trauma to a child that will plague them for the rest of their life. Such events will become the stuff of future nightmares and phobias. Most of the serious emotional wounds that a soul receives happen during childhood due to the soul's poor ability to process these events and cope with them.

I know a woman who is in her sixties. Recently, some traumatic events from her past have surfaced. She spends her days exploding in angry outbursts toward her relatives over wrongs that were done to her as a child. She continually relives the tragedies of her youth. Her life is a mess because she's never been healed of the emotional trauma that occurred during her childhood.

If you're a parent, it's important to take the fears your children express seriously. I'm not suggesting that you let a child run your home. I am suggesting that you refrain from minimizing the seriousness of their emotional reactions. Toddlers will resort to temper tantrums when they don't get their way. That's not what we're discussing. If a child displays a strong negative emotion— especially fear—toward a particular situation, it should be a red flag that warns you something is wrong. You might set time aside and ask what the child is feeling and let them know there is no need to be afraid. You might consider honoring their wishes if they are reasonable.

CHAPTER FOUR

The Development of Alternate Personalities

THE SOUL CAN PROCESS AND adapt to emotional trauma in a unique way. When an emotionally traumatic event is experienced, a part of the soul is wounded. When a part of the soul is injured, the wound may be walled-off or compartmentalized, similar to how the physical body creates a scab or scar tissue after physical trauma. The wounded part of the soul retains the memory and emotions related to the traumatic event. A traumatic event creates a part of the soul that is separated from the central part of the soul.

In communities where these matters are discussed, the main part of the soul is called the core. A wounded part of the soul that contains the memories and emotions of a traumatic event is called a fragment. Soul fragments may also be called "parts." Some soul fragments only retain memories and emotions from a single event. Others retain the memories and emotions of numerous similar events.

Because the soul generates our personality, a wounded part of the soul may develop its own persona. When a wounded part of the soul develops a unique persona, it is called an alter. (Alter is an abbreviation for alternate personality.) Like a fragment, an alter retains memories and emotions of specific events, but unlike fragments, they can have unique personalities that are distinctly different from the core personality.

A fragment or alter may go unnoticed until an event occurs that is reminiscent of the one that caused it to be created in the first place. When a similar event happens, the wounded part is triggered. When an alter or fragment is triggered, the individual's will and emotions come under its control. The person will then behave in correspondence to the personality of the alter, while the core personality remains passive. (If a fragment assumes control, they will react according to the memories and emotions retained by the fragment.)

When an alter or fragment assumes control of the individual's actions, the core persona may feel like an observer of what is happening rather than the one who is in control. Some describe it as like watching a stranger drive their car while they observe from the rear seat. When the core personality senses a disconnect from the physical world, it is known as dissociation. Often, the core personality is unaware of what is happening when an alter or fragment is in control. When the triggering event passes, and the core assumes control again, it's not unusual for them to have no recollection of what they said or did during the episode. This is common when the core persona is unaware of the alter's existence. If the alter and core are aware of each other and if they communicate, the core will generally remember what happened while the alter was in control.

A person with multiple alters that cause clinically significant problems may be diagnosed with D.I.D. (Dissociative Identity Disorder, formerly known as Multiple Personality Disorder). A severely traumatized person can have hundreds or even thousands of alters and fragments.

A person's alters may seem to have vastly different ages, and may even present themselves as different genders compared to the physical body. They may have other names, or no name at all. Alters may serve in different roles or functions, either related to daily life or managing the

The Development of Alternate Personalities

effects of trauma. They exhibit different moods, attitudes, and preferences for food and music. Each alter has a unique perception of their general appearance, i.e., hair color and length, skin color, eye color, body shape, etc. Alters each have unique memories; some remember events that others do not. They can have biological differences, i.e., different visual acuity, responses to medication, allergies, blood glucose levels, heart rate, blood pressure, immune function, EEG readings, etc. The physiological differences manifested in one body by different alters suggest that our emotional and spiritual states greatly influence our health. Typically, the core personality will take care of daily responsibilities such as shopping, cooking, parenting, working, gardening, paying bills, etc. One alter (or a group of them) will perform these tasks in some individuals. These parts do not usually retain traumatic memories and often have amnesia of traumatic events. Other alters are responsible for activities inside the soul. These alters retain memories of traumatic events.

A curious phenomenon must be considered with respect to alters, fragments, the memories they retain and the emotions they feel. One would think that the emotions related to traumatic events of which we are aware would be easily accessed, but this is not always true. It is common to know about a traumatic event and not be able to feel the expected emotion associated with it. Emotions connected to trauma are retained by alters and fragments that have their own will. They may choose not to allow access to an emotion. This leaves the individual with no ability to feel the expected emotion connected to an event. Similarly, if a memory is involved, and the alter refuses to make it known, the person will have no recollection of the event. It is common for an alter or fragment to retain the emotion or memory and not share it with the core personality until the alter or fragment has decided they are ready to be healed. Once this decision is made, the individual will suddenly feel the emotion that was absent. If a memory has been hidden, they will be able to recall the event.

The group of alters and fragments that inhabit the soul is referred to as a system. A system may contain a few alters and fragments, or it may be indescribably complex. Each person's system is unique to them. The simplicity or complexity of a system of alters and fragments is determined by the severity and frequency of trauma an individual has experienced.

Most people are not aware of the existence of alters and fragments. Those who have been Christians their entire lives may never have heard a discussion about this subject. Wounded parts of the soul are not discussed in most churches. The Bible (as far as they know) does not discuss alters and fragments. So, when the discussion involves a person coming under the control of another being, many Christians can only conceive of this "other being" as a demon. But alters and fragments are not demons.

Generally, only one persona will control the body at a time, but occasionally, two or more alters may share control. The individual's mood, behavior, preferences, and memories at any point in time are determined by the persona that is in control.

Some alters are formed as a defense mechanism against perceived threats. For example, when the soul faces what it believes to be a life or death situation, an alter may be formed that acts as a protector. A protecting alter may react differently to a threat than the core personality would. The alter may be more assertive, aggressive, or may resort to violence when it is not appropriate. Once the perceived threat has passed, the core resumes control and may have no memory of the event. When an alter assumes control or relinquishes it to another alter or the core, it is called *switching*.

I know a woman who has a terrible fear of going into basements. When I asked why she has this fear, she said it was because she had been molested by her uncles in a basement when she was a child. When she was molested, a part of her soul was wounded. The event created an alter whose dominant emotion is fear. Today, whenever she thinks about going into a basement, the alter is triggered. As the alter assumes control, she expresses fear that seems irrational to others. I suspect that most people have alters or fragments, though most of us are unaware of them. They're easiest to recognize when a person's behavior suddenly changes. Allow me to illustrate this idea further.

I once had a paramedic partner who was a Vietnam veteran. We worked in a part of town that was heavily populated with Vietnamese immigrants. In my time working with him, I noticed two things that seemed to trigger a sudden change in his behavior. One of them was going on a call at night to the home of a Vietnamese family. On these calls, he would become suspicious, agitated, and aggressive. After we left the home, his behavior would return to normal. It seems that an alter was created in response to traumatic events that happened when he was in Vietnam. When he was in a situation that reminded him of that time, the alter would perceive the environment as a threat and temporarily take over until the perceived threat had passed.

The other thing that triggered unusual behavior in my partner was fireworks. One year, we worked a standby event when the International Fireworks Convention was in town. That night, I sat in the ambulance and enjoyed the fireworks display. My partner spent the night lying on the gurney in the back of the ambulance with his hands covering his head, trembling in fear. Fireworks resemble the tracers and flares that soldiers use in combat. My partner had an alter that was triggered by fireworks. The alter assumed control, and he displayed what seemed to me to be irrational behavior. Once the fireworks were over, the alter relinquished control. The following story illustrates a more common way in which alters can be recognized.

Years ago, I spoke with a woman who vacations with her family on the Oregon coast. She said her husband always acted strangely while on these trips. According to her, from the time they began driving toward the beach, he would behave like a spoiled 13-year-old with a bad attitude. He would remain this way the entire time he was on vacation. But as soon as he returned home, his behavior returned to normal. His wife could not understand why he acted this way until she read a Facebook thread where I discussed alters and fragments. After reading my description of how wounded parts of the soul can cause people to exhibit Jekyll and Hyde-like behavior, she understood that her husband had an alter or fragment that caused him to behave this way. Her husband likely experienced an emotionally traumatic event on a trip to the coast as a teenager that created the alter or fragment. Once it was created, it reacted to events similar to the one that created it. Whenever he went to the coast, the alter perceived a threat. It then assumed control until he returned home and the perceived threat had passed.

One clue that you may have an alter or fragment being triggered is a tendency to react with a strong emotional response to minor incidents that would not cause others to react the same way. Many people experience chronic anxiety or panic attacks. Sometimes, the emotions of panic and anxiety are manifestations of an alter or fragment that has been triggered.

A second clue to the existence of an alter or fragment is when friends or family note that you exhibit sudden, dramatic changes in mood and behavior.

If you have gaps in your memory about specific events from the past that others remember, or if there are long gaps of time where you have no recollection of what happened to you, it may be due to the formation of alters or fragments. In these cases, wounded parts of the soul retain the memories of the events, and your core persona has no access to them. Some alters share memories with the core personality, but others do not. When an alter or fragment retains the only memory of an event, it leaves the individual with amnesia.

(The terms I use in this book to describe the parts of the soul are not universally accepted. Those who work in clinical settings may use different terms to describe these concepts. Emotional healing is a relatively new field of study. In time, new discoveries will be made that suggest better models of how the soul operates.)

CHAPTER FIVE

My Emotional Healing

Discussions with my friend Steve Harmon helped me learn the basics of emotional healing. As he shared his experiences, they made me realize that I needed emotional healing, too. From the stories that friends shared, I imagined emotional healing would take a great deal of time. I had also heard a few stories where well-meaning Christians tried to cast out alters as if they were demons. This caused me to be apprehensive about going through the process myself. After weighing all of this, I felt it was needed, but I only knew a few people I trusted to facilitate the process.

One day, I experienced a series of events at work that caused me to become angry. I had been assigned a new EMT partner. He had a way of doing his job that frustrated me. I often found myself becoming angry over the little things that he did. I wondered if perhaps God put us together to help me identify and deal with a problem.

The issues that caused me to become angry were minor. They would not normally cause a strong emotional reaction. I could see some of the events coming before they happened. I told myself I would not become angry. But as the events unfolded, I felt anger growing and spent most of the day in a sour mood. Fortunately, I was able to sit quietly in the ambulance for most of the day, and my anger didn't have an opportunity to hurt other people.

During this time, I spent many nights after work venting my frustrations to my wife, who is always sympathetic. One problem with having a supportive friend is that sometimes, they'll justify your sin. I had accepted people's justification for my moments of rage. But I felt like something was causing the anger that needed to be addressed. As I reflected on the angry outbursts, I realized they were all triggered by similar circumstances.

I remembered someone writing about emotional wounds and describing one of the symptoms: one sign that you have an emotional wound is when you overreact to a certain type of situation repeatedly. If you're an easy-going person who seldom gets angry and certain situations constantly trigger the same type of response—in this case, an overreaction of anger—there's an alter or fragment reacting to the situations.

I'd been having moments where a fragment of my soul was taking over and causing me to overreact in anger. I prayed for understanding. The Holy Spirit suggested that all of this was related to events that happened when I was a teenager. I finally accepted that I needed to be healed.

One day, my friend Matt Evans saw one of my posts on Facebook about my need for emotional healing. He sent me a text message asking if I had time to talk. We talked by phone the following day. During our conversation, he assisted me with emotional healing. The process we used is outlined below.

Sometimes, it helps if the wounded part of the soul is allowed to take temporary control of the mind, will, and emotions. This usually requires the individual to recall an event from the past that causes the emotion to be felt strongly. (In another chapter, we'll discuss emotional healing when you can't recall the event.) To receive healing, the wounded part of the soul must (in most cases) meet Jesus and receive healing and instruction from Him.

> 1. Matt asked me to recall an event where I could feel anger. This was easy to do. There were many events I could recall that brought up the emotion of anger. Matt had me remember one of the earliest events, and when I was feeling the emotion, he had me say a few short prayers that are listed below. He asked me to resist the temptation to overthink the situation. Healing the wounded soul is a purely emotional process. When you attempt to rationalize or think about what's happening, especially if you try to justify your feelings, it interferes with your ability to sense the emotions that need healing. He urged me not to overthink what we were doing.
>
> 2. I confessed to God that my anger was a sin. (Anger is not always a sin. This matter will be discussed in a later chapter.)
>
> 3. I said that I believed the blood of Jesus had taken away the penalty and consequences of my sin.
>
> 4. I asked Jesus to take away my anger.
>
> 5. We both felt like Jesus wanted to give me something in return for giving Him my anger. I felt as though he wanted to give me His peace. So, I asked him to give me His peace in exchange for my anger, and I received His peace.
>
> 6. I asked Jesus to heal the wound in my soul.
>
> 7. When we were done with this process. Matt asked me to recall one of the events again.

I was surprised when I tried to recall an event. I had difficulty seeing them in my mind and did not feel the anger. It was as if there had been an open door to the events that I could go through any time to access them, but after I went through the healing process, the door was no longer open. In fact, I couldn't even see the events. It seemed as if the events had never happened. The fact that I could no longer access the events or feel the emotions of anger led me to believe I was healed.

This is not to say that I would never again get angry. That's not how emotional healing works. It doesn't take away your ability to feel certain emotions. It merely heals the wounded parts of the soul that are dominated by negative emotions.

I received a strange confirmation the following day. When I arrived at work, my EMT partner informed me that he was being transferred to another unit. I couldn't help but think that God had finally accomplished what he wanted with this partner, and it was time for a new one.

CHAPTER SIX

A Simple Approach to Emotional Healing

AFTER I RECEIVED EMOTIONAL HEALING, I decided to use the same approach with a few of my patients. One day, I transported a woman who had been admitted to a hospital for homicidal ideation. She was consumed with rage and attempted to kill her husband. While transporting her to a psychiatric facility, I asked if she would be willing to participate in an experiment. I thought she would be healed if she gave her anger to Jesus and asked Him to heal her emotional wounds. She agreed to give it a try. I helped her with the process, and in a few minutes, her anger was gone. I used the same approach with other patients and saw similar results. I had found a process that worked.

Dozens of approaches to emotional healing have been developed to date. Each method has strengths and weaknesses. Some can be done quickly. Others take weeks or months. Some require extensive training to master. This chapter offers an approach to healing simple emotional trauma—the kind experienced by most people. Other chapters provide instruction for healing complex trauma— the kind experienced by ritual abuse survivors. The process I recommend is quick, effective, and can be done without the need for special training. Here are the basic steps I use for healing simple emotional trauma:

1. Recall an event from the past that causes a strong negative emotion when you think of it.
2. Identify the emotion(s) you feel.
3. Ask Jesus to take the emotion(s) from you.
4. Ask Him to heal the wound(s) in your soul.
5. Tell Him you receive His healing.

An optional step is asking Jesus to give you a positive emotion when He removes a negative one. Ask Him to give you joy when He removes sadness, love when He removes hate, or acceptance when He removes a feeling of rejection.

After you've done this once, recall the event again and see if a negative emotion remains. If so, it will likely not be the same emotion, but a *different* emotion related to the event. Work through that negative emotion by repeating the steps.

1. Identify the emotion(s) you feel.
2. Ask Jesus to take the emotion(s) from you.
3. Ask Him to heal the wound(s) in your soul.
4. Tell Him you receive His healing.

Allow a minute to pass and recall the event again. If a different emotion is present, repeat the process one more time and give that emotion to Jesus. If a negative emotion is not present, you are healed of the trauma from that event. Consider starting the process again using a different event that evokes a negative emotion. Continue using this process until all the trauma during your life has been healed. In many cases, mysterious illnesses and pains that have not responded to prayer will spontaneously resolve.

If you are troubled by a negative emotion such as guilt, shame, or anger but cannot recall an event associated with it, omit step number one

A Simple Approach to Emotional Healing

from the list above. Simply identify the emotion you feel and give it to Jesus, then repeat as needed.

I'm sometimes asked if we can be healed of more than one emotion at a time. Generally, the emotions of a particular event, though different in nature, can be addressed simultaneously. For example, anger, fear, and hopelessness related to a single traumatic event may be healed at once. Sometimes, Jesus will heal one emotion from different events at the same time. I've also received testimonies from people who have had a variety of emotions from different events healed simultaneously, as related by Paula:

> Yesterday, I was thinking about my mom, who passed away in 2020. Mom and I always had a strained relationship. I believe she was bipolar as she had horrible mood swings that had my siblings, me, and my dad, always in an upheaval. Mom was a believer in Christ and made sure us kids went to church regularly. Once, I told her she needed help and why not try a therapist. She refused, saying Jesus is my therapist. She wasn't crazy every day, but more often than not. Every now and then, a memory of some horrible thing she did or said would surface and blow my day completely.
>
> Yesterday, a memory surfaced of one incident that was particularly bad. I thought to myself, I'm sick of these memories that occasionally pop up. I went through the steps of emotional healing, but this time, I asked Jesus to take all negative emotions from all of these memories at once instead of one or two that occasionally pop up. I realized I have a tendency to hang on to these, and I gave that to Jesus too.
>
> Later, a friend and old childhood neighbor sent me a link to an old school song, "Just a Closer Walk with Thee" by Patti Page. As I listened to it, I remembered hearing Mom singing this in the kitchen while canning vegetables. I was flooded with good memories. It actually felt like my mom was there with me. I envisioned my mom and Jesus standing there smiling and knew the bad emotions from the bad memories had finally come to a close. This was a new memory—a good one. And the song made me weep.

Some have found that if you find the first occurrence of a negative emotion and heal the wound associated with it, the individual will be healed of all other wounds connected to that emotion. Jesus will use different approaches with different people for reasons only He knows.

CHAPTER SEVEN

Emotional Healing: The Long Path

IT CAN TAKE LESS THAN a minute to heal the wound caused by an emotionally traumatic event. However, most people experience trauma over their entire lifetime. Healing hundreds (or thousands) of emotional wounds may take time. Whether we decide to take the time required to receive healing of many wounds or only a few is up to us. The following testimony was submitted by someone who wanted to be completely healed of her traumatic past. (Her name has been withheld by request.)

> Dear PM,
>
> After we came across your Q decodes in 2018, I noticed you had some spiritual videos on your website too, so I started listening to them. I came across one where you were teaching a group of women about emotional healing and had a volunteer stand up with her emotional issue that she wanted healing from. I think somewhere you recommended starting with the oldest negative memory we can think of. So, I started there.

39

EMOTIONAL HEALING AND DELIVERANCE MADE SIMPLE

My oldest memory was from when I was quite young (I grew up in a 5th world country), seeing a dog being stoned to death because it had rabies. It was pretty traumatic. I also dealt with fears of snakes, dogs, rushing rivers, bears, panthers, monkeys, and so on. Those were not phobias. Real issues. I was sent off to boarding school when I was 11 and only saw my parents between semesters after that. I was an extreme introvert, and being "all alone" in a different country was very traumatic for me. Most of my issues stem back to that time. Tons of insecurities, not feeling good enough, and not feeling attractive. There was no abuse or drugs or anything people might think necessary for a need for emotional healing. I was quite messed up.

After years of these emotions ruling my life with jealousies, the need to control, depression, and not being able to open up to people, I began to work on 50 years of emotions one by one. It took a lot of time, but I was very motivated. I could see that it worked! I think I have gotten through most everything in the past, but I use it almost daily for staying clear of any negative emotions as they come up in daily life. If I feel less than clean of negative feelings, I try to root out what it is I'm feeling and deal with it immediately. It is so freeing, and I am a new person! I never thought I could be free of jealousy and insecurity!

There is another piece to the healing puzzle. I began recording my dreams three years ago because of you. I didn't have decoding help right at the beginning, but you had said that sometimes the message may be in the meaning of the name. I could easily find out the name meanings. He showed me His love by calling me names! Beloved, Dearly loved, Precious, A joyous song, Small strong woman, One who wields a battle sword, The source of a Father's joy, Warrior, Treasured jewel, One who is bound to God. Once I was able to understand some of the dreams He sent me now and then, showing His love for me in actions, showing that He notices me and cares for me. He has been very patient and tender with me. He is my very beloved God!

It's easy to dismiss dreams as pointless meanderings of the soul. But I've learned that God will hide messages in dreams that seem irrelevant. Sometimes, God will show us His love. Other times, we'll be given instruction, or meet alters or fragments that need healing.

CHAPTER EIGHT

Overnight Healing

IN THE PREVIOUS CHAPTER, WE read about a woman who committed herself to a lengthy process of healing. While it may take time to be healed of a lifetime of trauma, there are exceptions. One can be healed of multiple injuries and severe trauma in a short period of time. The following testimony submitted by a man named David is an example of how God can instantly heal us of a lifetime of trauma and injury.

> As a child, I was abused by my father. Beaten, degraded, humiliated, and forced to eat my own feces on several occasions. At the age of 19, I was in a house fire and burned over 80 percent of my body. I recovered physically, although scarred, but mentally, I remained damaged. I began drinking at the age of 13. While in the hospital, due to extreme weight loss, I was given not only beer but all the morphine and Percocet a body could take. I went in an alcoholic and became a drug addict while I was there. Before being discharged, I was detoxed from the drugs. The drinking continued until I was 21, when I was truly born again at Church on the Rock in Fort Myers, Florida.

EMOTIONAL HEALING AND DELIVERANCE MADE SIMPLE

At 23, I was recruited by John Jacob's and the Power Team. Due to not dealing with my mental health issues, I walked away from God and the Church. I went on with life working as a prison guard and private investigator, collecting debts, repossessing cars, and, as I know now, collecting more and more demons. I was drinking heavily, abusing steroids, and destroying the relationships in my life. Over the years, I have hurt so many people even though I always attempted to do the right thing. Over the past few years, I have rekindled my relationship with God. Still, I continued to do the wrong things. I simply had no control. Last week, my wife kicked me out and placed a restraining order on me. She is filing for divorce Tuesday. The past week, I have struggled greatly with suicide. I put a nine millimeter gun to my head, but stopped. I considered getting a bottle of insulin from work and shooting it all. It would be easy to do as I am now a nurse. The only thing that stopped me was what it would do to my mother.

I have followed you for some time on Telegram. I enjoy reading your posts but never watched your videos. Last night, for some reason, I clicked on one of your video links to Emotional Healing. I prayed the prayers with you and sincerely meant every word. I got on my knees and asked God to heal me. I realized my soul had truly been torn and shattered. When I got off my knees, I felt nothing. I went to bed and prayed myself to sleep.

I woke today, and truly feel like a new person. Not only was the darkness gone, but I truly feel peace and joy even though my marital life is a mess. Not only did God heal my soul, but he also healed my body. A lifetime of power-lifting, fights, and general abuse left me with two torn rotator cuffs that gave me chronic pain. God heard my cries, and he healed me. I have upcoming appointments with doctors and a therapist that I am going to follow through with. I never could speak of the things I have been through, but finally, I have found the strength and courage. I have always been hesitant to discuss my life as well. The entire story is so wild it sounds like an outlandish lie.

God heard me and healed me. Watching that video saved my life. I am fully submitting myself to God. I am now praying that God will also soften the heart of my wife and heal this marriage.

CHAPTER NINE

Yelena's Healing

IN THIS CHAPTER, I'LL SHARE a testimony of how I helped a woman receive healing from emotional trauma while transporting her by ambulance from a hospital to a mental health facility.

I stood at the nurse's station reading my patient's chart as her nurse cared for another patient. Looking at the hospital's personal information sheet, I noticed that she was born in Romania and that she was a Christian. My partner, who is more curious than me, went into the patient's room. Glancing at her history and physical, I saw that she had fibromyalgia and multiple injuries from a car accident, which required extensive physical therapy. She suffered from depression and had a long list of prescription medications. The physician who wrote the report also noted that she used a walker. My partner came out of her room. I asked if she spoke with an accent. "Not that I can tell," he replied. "She sounds like everyone else."

After receiving a verbal report about the patient from her nurse, I entered her room. We talked for a few minutes, but I couldn't detect even the slightest trace of an accent. "You must have moved to the States when you were very young," I said.

"Actually, I moved here when I was fifteen."

"Really? So, what happened to your Romanian accent?" I held out the hospital information sheet and pointed to the line where it lists her country of birth.

"Oh, that," she said with a smile that lasted only a moment. "After I moved here, I was beaten every day in school because of my accent. I figured I could avoid being beaten if I learned to speak perfect English. Ten years after moving here, my English was so good I got a job teaching English."

Yelena had a good sense of humor. We joked with each other as we helped her to the gurney. After securing her personal belongings, including her walker, we wheeled her toward the elevator. As we drove toward our destination, the conversation became more serious. Sensing that she had been through a lot of abuse, I asked about her past.

She told me about being beaten and raped many times as a child—once by a man she later learned was her father. "As I got older, I became interested in gymnastics. I was really good and started to do well in competitions. This made my father so mad he tried to kill me by throwing me in front of a train. I thought I could leave it all behind by moving to the United States, but somehow the problems followed me."

She talked about how her husband abused her and then about the day he took her to church, and the pastor gave a message that cut her to the heart. She got saved that day and asked her husband if he told the pastor about her life. He had not. The Holy Spirit gave the pastor a message that seemed to be just for her.

Later, she was drugged and raped by a man and his wife. Yelena's husband blamed her for it, saying it was her choice to meet with them. She said that although it was a blessing that her husband got her saved, he had been a terrible husband. After she was disabled in a car accident and went through physical therapy, he began stealing her pain pills and became addicted to them. His addiction made him more violent toward her. From her perspective, things couldn't get any worse.

Seeing all this pain and trauma, I felt it was time to bring Jesus into the meeting. I looked into her eyes and said, "You know what? I have a way to get you healed of the painful emotions from all that abuse."

"And how are you going to do that?" she asked.

"Jesus is going to do it."

A smile appeared on her face. "I know all about Jesus... I'm a Christian."

"I know you are," I replied. "But you don't know how badly He wants to heal you, so let me share a couple of stories." I told her about how my emotional trauma was healed and shared a few other testimonies. "Most people know that the Bible says by His stripes, we are healed, but the Bible also says He bore our griefs and sorrows. All your grief, all your sorrow, and all those painful memories were taken by Him on the cross. And if He already bore them for you, then you don't need to bear them anymore." She was excited about the possibility of being healed by Jesus. "I can help get you healed, Yelena. All we need to do is let Jesus take away the painful emotions. If you're ready, I will ask you to remember the most painful memory you have."

"I'm ready."

Her most painful memory was connected to the time she was drugged and raped. It wasn't the incident itself that troubled her. She had little memory of what happened. What bothered her was the fact that her husband blamed her for it. I asked her to recall a time when her husband said it was her fault, then asked what emotion she felt.

"Guilt."

"Yelena, repeat after me. Jesus, I ask you to take this guilt from me and heal the wound in my soul." She repeated what I said and began crying, so I gave her a minute to compose herself before continuing. When she was ready, I continued. "Okay, let's do it one more time. There you are with your husband in another argument about the time you were drugged and raped. He tells you it's all your fault. What is the strongest negative emotion you feel?"

She began crying again. "Shame."

I had her give the feeling of shame to Jesus. When she stopped crying, I said we need to do it one more time. I rehearsed the scene with her husband accusing her. "What emotion do you feel this time?"

With her mouth hanging open in amazement, she said, "Nothing. Nothing at all. I can remember all the times he accused me, but I don't feel the pain anymore. It's gone."

"That's because Jesus healed you. Yelena, you're going to be spending a few days going through treatment. It might be a good idea to let Jesus heal the rest of those wounds while you're there. You can do the same thing we just did by yourself. Bring up any painful memories, identify the emotions you feel, and ask Jesus to take them from you."

We arrived at the mental health facility and unloaded the gurney. She got off and got in line at the registration desk. Before we left, she gave me a hug and thanked me.

CHAPTER TEN

Are You Ready To Be Healed?

HEALING IS A GIFT FROM God. Because it is a gift, we must be willing to receive it. Although healing is available to everyone, some are able to receive it more readily than others. If one is not interested in emotional healing, they will not engage in the process and won't receive it. Not everyone is ready for healing at the same point in time. Occasionally, our soul must be prepared first. Preparation seems to involve the agitation of negative emotions. I'm uncertain as to the cause of this stirring of emotions. It's possible that it is done by God, but I have no way to confirm that.

One clue that you are ready for emotional healing is an increase in the frequency of uncomfortable emotions. Before my first experience with emotional healing, I experienced frequent outbursts of anger. That was the sign that I was ready to be healed. A woman named Lindsay experienced a similar phenomenon, which she explains in her testimony:

EMOTIONAL HEALING AND DELIVERANCE MADE SIMPLE

I had been experiencing anger and anxiety building in my life for no reason. It's been getting worse, and I have been asking Jesus to heal my soul, set me free, and show me what it is, so I can let it go. I have small children, and it was affecting my parenting and patience for a couple of years now. I recently seemed to take a turn for the worse and questioned God's desire or ability to truly help me be free. I am a spirit-filled believer who often works through inner healing and deliverance. I couldn't believe I was dealing with this.

Well, last night, I couldn't stop feeling this upwelling of emotion when I got home after attending alcoholics anonymous. When I went to wash my face after giving the kids a bath, I saw Jesus. I knew he was telling me it was time. I sat on the toilet, locked the door, and began to cry into a towel. I couldn't stop sobbing. Suddenly, I knew as a child, I was so angry at my mom and at my dad too. I was continuously "abandoned" as a small child by my mother. Every one of my attached caregivers I've loved or felt safe with had abandoned me or let me down as a small and growing child. I finally felt all the grief, pain, and anger. That's where my anger comes from. I'm so angry at my mom. Even though I've done years of forgiveness and have a relationship with her now, there was a soul wound that would only be healed by His spirit. Not by might, not in my own power, but by His Spirit.

I realized the whole time I was experiencing this with Holy Spirit, I felt Jesus and the Father holding me and speaking the word, "truth," over me. "I'll never leave you nor forsake you. You were fearfully and wonderfully made. You are not broken. You are loved. The lies that I believed were broken." He is not going to desert me if I make a mistake. He will never leave me. Even if I make my bed in Sheol, the place of the dead, he will be there.

I felt so much better. The tightness and anger are gone this morning. I've asked him to replace the space in my soul with these truths permanently. He is so faithful.

In most cases, emotional healing is a simple process. No assistance is needed, and no formal training is required. Our next testimony is from Nikki Beck, whose baby was diagnosed with a fatal condition prior to birth and placed on hospice before being delivered.

Hi Dave,

I was just listening to your podcast about upcoming books and wanted to share about my first experience with emotional healing. I have shared your information about emotional healing many times with many people and have shared my testimony in church many times over the years.

In 2004, I was pregnant and found out that our daughter, Sydney Faith, had Trisomy 18, which we were told was incompatible with life. Unfortunately, I was not aware of how much God still heals today at that time, and I didn't have the faith to believe for anything other than what we were told. My prayers that I did ask for were answered. She was born alive; we got to spend some time with her, she didn't appear to suffer, and it was a beautiful day.

She was on hospice while I was still pregnant, and we planned to take her home as soon as we were allowed—which was 4 hours after she was born. As we were leaving the hospital, she was fading, and she died in my arms in front of the hospital. We took her home. Some family came to see her and say their final goodbyes. When everyone left, and it was just my husband and I with the hospice nurse, she contacted a funeral home that was coming to take her body so she could be cremated. When they arrived, we carried her out to the minivan, and she opened the van door and there was a Rubbermaid storage tote... to put our baby girl in... it wrecked us. We just lost it, weeping, falling to my knees... it was so traumatic.

Years later, when talking about that moment, it would take me there again, and I would experience that same pain. It would take my breath away. I had been following you on Facebook. After hearing you talk about how to pray for emotional healing, I decided to try it. I skipped church that day and had a date with God on my front porch to give it a try. It was emotional, partially because I think I might have wanted to hold onto that pain, feeling like, as a mom who lost her baby, I should be that upset... but regardless, I went through the emotional healing prayer and experienced healing from that trauma. I can talk about it now without losing my breath and feeling that pain. Since then, I've used your method to walk my children, sister, mother, and friends through emotional healing. Thank you so much for your ministry and sharing your gift by simplifying powerful praying.

With much love and gratitude,
Nikki Beck

It's not uncommon to believe we have been healed of the pain of a traumatic event, only to have the negative emotion hit us once again as we retell the story. Unfortunately, we may have been simply distracting ourselves by trying to push forward. It has been said that when you can

EMOTIONAL HEALING AND DELIVERANCE MADE SIMPLE

tell the story, and it doesn't hurt, you know you have been healed. My friend Andy relates one such story in the following testimony:

> After more or less begging God for children for about 20 years, I met my wife, Amber, and two years later, she became pregnant. Amazingly we were given a prophetic word by a friend that an upcoming date would be significant for us, and that was the day we found out she was pregnant. About six weeks later, Amber began to have complications. To make a long story short, six emergency room visits and two surgeries later, we lost our baby, whom we affectionately named "Guppy." As if all the emergency room visits and surgeries weren't enough, the loss of the baby I had prayed for, for all those years was somehow taken from us. We were completely grief-stricken, but I refused to blame God or stay "stuck" in the swamp of questions and despair. Just a couple of years prior, another very traumatic event had happened in my life that lasted a year and a half. During that time, I learned to navigate loss and "turn my mourning into praise," as the Bible says. During that time, I believed the grief from the loss wasn't going to be any different, but perhaps it would be easier to come out of.
>
> A few months passed, and I was totally confident that I had come out of that time of deep sadness and was emotionally free from any hurt associated with that time. I still had many of the "why" and "how" questions, but I didn't blame God for what had happened. Then one day, I joined in on one of Dave's live streams, and when it was my turn, I asked him something like, "What do you do with those times that you pray and things don't turn out like you believed they would?" I was surprised as I choked up as I tried to get out the words that Amber and I had lost our baby. I thought I was past it already. But when I finally did get the words out, Dave took me through the steps of emotional healing. It is no exaggeration when I say that within a minute, I went from feeling devastated when recounting the memory to him, to feeling joyful when recounting the memory. Now, that doesn't mean that I was happy that we lost our baby. No, instead, I am joyful and excited to meet our child in heaven someday, and over a year later, that is still what I think about. I no longer count the miscarriage as a loss but as something we gained but was sown into the future. As if going to heaven isn't enough, now I have someone waiting for me when I get there whom I've never met, and yet, love dearly.

Healing emotional trauma is not an exact science. There is much about the field that is not yet understood, but a few principles are clear. One of them is the fact that we are not all ready to receive healing at the same time. The soul must be prepared first. Once a wounded part of the soul is ready to be healed, if we engage the process, we will be healed.

CHAPTER ELEVEN

A Firefighter Healed of PTSD

I RECEIVED AN E-MAIL FROM a man named José, who is a missionary to Uganda. He had read several of my books and wanted to know if I might help his son—a paramedic firefighter who developed post-traumatic stress disorder (PTSD) and could no longer work. José said he would be in our area for a few weeks and asked if I would meet with him and his son for prayer. I agreed, and we set up a time to meet at a city park.

The day we agreed to meet had arrived. I parked and walked toward a picnic table where two men were sitting, one older and one younger. They got up as they saw me approaching. We shook hands and introduced ourselves, then sat down at the table. José thanked me for coming to meet with them. His son, David, and I talked for 20 minutes about his work as a paramedic and his separation from the fire department due to PTSD. I explained my process for emotional healing and asked if he wanted to give it a try. He agreed. I explained that I needed him to recall some of the more painful events from his career.

"Where do you want to start?" he asked.

"It doesn't matter," I said. "Just pick a call you went on that's especially painful when you think about it."

"I was working on the engine one night, and we went on this call for a motor vehicle accident. It never should have happened. The kid was just being stupid. He went out and got drunk. Then he drove his car into a tree. I was first on scene. The car was ripped in half, and he was lying there a bloody mess. There was nothing we could do to save him."

"Okay, David, as you think about this call, what emotion is the strongest?"

His eyes searched the trees behind me. "Grief. Just a lot of grief for his family."

"Okay, just repeat everything I say. Jesus, I ask you to take this grief from me. I don't want it anymore. I ask you to heal the wound in my soul. I receive your healing. In place of grief, I ask you to give me peace." Sentence by sentence, he repeated everything I said. "Okay, now I want you to think about the call one more time. You're on the engine responding to the call. You arrive on scene and find the car ripped in half and this dead kid there. What emotion do you feel now?"

"Sadness. Just a lot of deep sadness."

"Okay, repeat after me again: Jesus, I ask you to take this sadness from me. I don't want it anymore. I ask you to heal the wound in my soul from it. I receive your healing. In place of sadness, I ask you to give me joy." He repeated my words again. "Okay, now I want you to think about the call again. You arrive on scene and find the car torn in half and this dead kid there. What emotion do you feel now?"

David looked down for a moment, then looked up at me. "Nothing. The sadness and grief are gone. I don't feel anything. Maybe a sense of peace."

"It's pretty simple, isn't it?" I asked. "Isn't Jesus awesome?"

"Yes, he is."

"I want you to remember another call you went on that is especially painful when you think about it."

"It was Christmas day, and I was on the engine again. We responded to this house. The family had gathered for the holidays, and the grandfather tripped and fell. His knee came down on this baby's head and squashed it like a football. The parents were crying, and there was a lot of emotion. I knew the kid was dead, and there was nothing we could do to help them. But I told the family I would start an IV, and we would do what we could."

"As you think about this call, what emotion do you feel?"

"Grief. Just a lot of grief for the family."

"Okay, Jesus, I ask you to take this grief from me." He repeated what I said. "I ask you to heal the wound in my soul. I receive your healing. In place of grief, I ask you to give me joy." He repeated my words again. "Okay, now I want you to think about the call again. You arrive on scene and find this dead kid. What emotion do you feel?"

"Nothing. Nothing at all. I can't believe it. Is it really that easy?" He asked, smiling.

We spent about 30 minutes recalling one event after another, identifying the painful emotions, and giving them to Jesus. I explained that the process was simple enough that he could do it without me. I encouraged him to continue recalling painful events from the past and giving the emotions to Jesus. I explained that it works on present emotions as well as ones from the past. "It's hard to go through life without becoming offended or hurt by the things people say. If we allow things to wound us, it gives the enemy a place to attack us. But if we give the emotions to Jesus right away, it keeps us at peace. As soon as you recognize a new emotional wound, you might ask Jesus to take the painful emotion and heal you."

I asked David if he had any physical pain he wanted to be healed of. "Yeah, both of my shoulders are sore all the time. I think I might have torn rotator cuffs."

"Have you had an MRI yet?"

"Not yet. But I know the symptoms."

I had him stand up. "Raise your left arm out to your side as high as you can until you feel pain." He raised his arm a little higher than 90 degrees, then put it back down. I placed my hand on his left shoulder. "Holy Spirit, bring your power and presence. I command ligaments, nerves, tendons, bones, muscles, and cartilage to be healed in the name of Jesus. Spirit of pain, I command you to leave. Lord, I thank you for your healing." I asked him to raise his arm again. He was able to raise it straight up without any pain.

He began laughing. "Are you kidding me? That's amazing."

"Now, let's do the other one." I had to pray over his right shoulder four times before all the pain left. We sat down at the table again and talked about the power and authority God granted to us as believers. I brought along a copy of my book *Divine Healing Made Simple*. I handed it to him and told him he might want to begin reading it if he wanted to know more about healing.

"My dad told me a lot about you. I really want to start living the supernatural life. Thanks for the book. I'm definitely going to start reading it."

"You do that. And if you ever have any questions, you know how to get a hold of me." It was getting late, and I needed to get back home. We got up from the table. I gave José and David a hug. They went to their truck, and I got in my Jeep. I love seeing people healed, but there was something special about being able to help a fellow paramedic who has been through the same kind of trauma I've been through. It was an afternoon I won't forget.

CHAPTER TWELVE

A Healing Dialogue with God

I AM OFTEN ASKED WHAT words should be said or what actions should be taken to heal a certain condition. The question arises out of a belief that it is a precise set of words or a particular action that causes healing to occur. In some cases, a particular command or action *will* bring healing or remove an evil spirit. We intuitively know this to be true, at least in some cases. We want to know the magic words, so we can say them, be healed, and get on with life. For many people, the goal is to be healed as quickly and as efficiently as possible.

I often use a script for emotional healing. I've found that if I have an individual say certain words, they will be healed. And while a script can be used, it may turn healing into a mechanical process. Healing is not merely a means to rid ourselves of a problem. It is also an opportunity to develop a deep, personal relationship with God. I don't think it would be untrue to say that God is more interested in communicating with us than in healing our headaches. We were created for that very purpose; God is chiefly interested in developing a loving relationship with us. If we rely exclusively on a script, we may negate the relational aspect of healing.

The following testimony explains how one person was healed through their daily conversations with God.

> Right off the bat, I must admit that I feel like a hypocrite. My testimony is about being healed from a specific anxiety, and yet I still occasionally have some. Only it is much, much less, thanks to the Lord's healing power. Even if the healing is not yet complete, Jesus deserves to be glorified.
>
> **The Occasion:** A couple of years ago, my eye doctor recommended cataract surgery. Since I also have Fuchs corneal dystrophy, the surgery would be riskier the longer I waited. It would also make the dystrophy worse. If I did nothing, I could become blind like my mother did; she never had the surgery because she was terrified of it.
>
> I seemed to have inherited her fear, for I was petrified. Even though the surgery was still several weeks away, I was so gripped by anxiety that I couldn't function. Nothing helped except canceling the appointment—which wasn't a long-term solution, of course.
>
> In the past few months, the Lord has led me through a process of inner healing regarding this anxiety. As I mentioned above, it still raises its ugly head every so often, but where it was a constant 10 before, it is now a sporadic 3 or 4. And each spike is usually a sign that the Lord wants to go deeper and heal another aspect or level.
>
> **The Approach:** The Lord leads each of us differently. In this season of my life, I don't have any Christian brothers or sisters around me who can minister to me in the power of the Holy Spirit. It's just the Lord and me, and any books or videos He leads me to. For me, the key to being healed was being able to hear the Lord speak to me despite my anxiety. This meant approaching the subject step by little step, lest I become overwhelmed by my fears and shut Him out.
>
> He started by teaching me how to calm down and perceive His loving presence. I believe that we cannot hear Him unless we perceive His presence. It's not that He is absent or silent; He is always with us and He's always willing to talk. The problem lies on my end. When I'm gripped by anxiety or another strong emotion, it is impossible for me to hear Him. That's why I needed to learn to calm down and connect with Him first.

A Healing Dialogue with God

The next step was believing that God wanted to engage in a dialogue with me. Like most Christians, I usually talked and seldom listened. There had been times when I was able to hear Him, but they seemed few and far between. After a time of seeking Him about this, He showed me how easy the dialogue was. Through an online testimony, Jesus was saying, in effect, "Just ask me an open-ended question and pay attention to the thought that comes to you after 10-15 seconds. If it lines up with Scripture and you have My peace, accept it and ask Me the next question."

As I began practicing the dialogue with Jesus, both in my journal during my morning prayer time and at other times during the day, I became more familiar with His voice. Again, I'm not perfect yet in that area, either, but I'm miles ahead of where I was just a few weeks ago. Being able to dialogue with Jesus about my anxieties became the key to my emotional healing.

He encouraged me to talk to Him about my fears as they arose. I sensed that He was listening without judging me in any way; on the contrary, He was glad to be with me and eager to help me. I would formulate my concern as a question and listen to His answer. Pretty soon, the dialogue would take off, and He would ask me a question in return or tell me to turn to a particular Scripture, which He then explained to me. Over a period of several weeks, this process would repeat several mornings a week as new concerns arose. Little by little, my anxieties subsided until I was able to make another appointment for surgery, this time without fear. So far, I've been mostly calm. This is not the supernatural calm that the Lord sometimes grants in an emergency, but the peace that comes from being healed emotionally.

The Process: I don't think the process is finished yet. For one thing, I'm still occasionally having the jitters, as I mentioned above. But even more importantly, I believe the Lord is interested in healing far more areas emotionally than just this one specific anxiety. I've been reading, *"Broken to Whole: Inner Healing for the Fragmented Soul,"* by Seneca Schurbon et. al. It contains far more material than I can process all at once, yet the Lord already used some of it to go deeper and touch some root causes of this and other anxieties.

I see my experience as a gateway to further emotional healing and a deeper walk with the Lord.

CHAPTER THIRTEEN

Removing Evil Spirits

SOME FIND IT HARD TO imagine that a demon could influence them. Outside of the church, the idea is considered a myth—a convenient excuse to shirk responsibility for our shortcomings. I'd like you to engage in a thought experiment. It is generally understood that the human soul is the seat of the mind, will, and emotions. Our will is our capacity to choose.

Have you ever made a choice not to do something and then, after a mental struggle, gave in and did it anyway?

If our will is under our complete control, why do we struggle to bring our actions under the control of our will?

Why does it seem that sometimes we battle against an invisible force that opposes our will?

EMOTIONAL HEALING AND DELIVERANCE MADE SIMPLE

What exactly is this invisible force?

The answer to these questions varies depending on whom you ask. I've found that the biblical explanation comports most accurately with reality. The Bible describes humans as three-part beings.

> *Now may the God of peace Himself sanctify you completely; and may your whole spirit, soul, and body be preserved blameless at the coming of our Lord Jesus Christ.*
> 1 THESS. 5:23

We are triune beings that exist in two different realms: the physical universe and its spiritual counterpart. One cannot experience the spiritual dimension through the senses of the physical body. It is experienced by our spirit. The spiritual universe is divided into two domains—the kingdom of heaven and the kingdom of darkness. God is the ruler of the kingdom of heaven. He desires to influence the universe toward His perfect will. Satan rules the kingdom of darkness. He intends to bring the universe under submission to his will. God and Satan do not exert direct control over inhabitants of the physical world. Instead, they advance their kingdoms by influencing human spirits. Whether knowingly or in ignorance, we carry out their will on the earth.

We may choose to cooperate with the Spirit of God and angels. The Holy Spirit guides our spirit and attempts to align our thoughts, words, and actions with heaven's agenda. Similarly, evil spirits may attempt to sway us. They hope to compel us to carry out Satan's agenda. Invisible spirits of one kind or another try continually to influence us.

Evil spirits do not have physical bodies, as we do, but spiritual ones. Despite this, they desire to impact the physical world. Their ability to interact in the physical dimension is limited, so they use humans to accomplish their agenda. They do so by exerting influence over our mind, will, and emotions. The apostle Paul suggested that emotions like anger provide an opportunity for demons to influence us.

> *"In your anger do not sin": Do not let the sun go down while you are still angry, and do not give the devil a foothold.*
> EPH. 4:26-27 NIV

Removing Evil Spirits

Anger is not always sinful. Jesus became angry at the moneychangers and drove them out of the temple. His anger was justified because the moneychangers charged unfair prices to those who wanted to be reconciled to God.

The Apostle Paul warned against allowing anger to fester. If a situation arises that causes anger, deal with the issue quickly and release the anger. Emotions like anger may compel you to take needed action or they may create opportunities for evil spirits to influence our souls and afflict our physical bodies.

How does a demon do this?

One way is by tormenting the alters and fragments that are created by emotional trauma. When we heal alters and fragments, we remove the access point for demons.

I want to address a point of contention about the way demons affect humans. Many Bible translations use the word *possess* to describe the way demons influence us. The English Bible's descriptions of people being demon-possessed are a mistranslation. When the Greek text of the New Testament is correctly translated, the term "demon-possessed" is not found. Instead, three other terms are used. Some passages say, "to have a demon." Others say, "to be in a demon." The most common term is "demonized." These three terms mean essentially the same thing and are used interchangeably in the account of the man with the demon named "Legion" (see Matt 8:28-34; Mark 5:1-20; Luke 8:26-39). None of these terms indicates total ownership or control of an individual. They simply mean that the individual is affected or influenced by a demon.

What most people think of as demonic possession is merely a demon exerting more influence over its host at a particular point in time. Evil spirits can go unnoticed for long periods of time and then suddenly assume control of a physical body. Usually, when this occurs, the individual will shake or convulse uncontrollably. This manifestation typically lasts only a few minutes, and then, the person resumes control of their body. Note that I called this a manifestation. When a spirit being—whether a demon, angel or the Spirit of God—makes its presence known in the physical world, it is referred to as a manifestation.

EMOTIONAL HEALING AND DELIVERANCE MADE SIMPLE

Demons manifest control over a physical body for only a short period of time before relinquishing control back to their host.

A popular teaching among Christians asserts that those who are born again by the Spirit of God cannot be possessed by demons. The rationale is that God's Spirit and a demon cannot occupy the same body. While the idea sounds logical on its face, it has several flaws.

When one is born again by the Spirit of God, their spirit (not their soul) is regenerated or made new. It is in the human spirit where the life of God resides. Demons do not affect our spirit. They influence our soul. Thus, we can be influenced both by the Spirit of God and evil spirits. A second error involves the idea of possession. As mentioned previously, demons do not "possess" human bodies. They exert influence over the soul and afflict the physical body with sickness.

Those who claim Christians cannot be possessed by demons teach that when believers exhibit demonic behavior, it is not possession but *oppression*. A doctrine has been developed that says non-believers may be possessed, but believers cannot be. Some teach that such demonic "oppression" may need prayer but not deliverance. Demonization is not a binary matter of possession for non-believers and oppression for believers. Demonic influence occurs on a spectrum from minor to severe without respect to one's salvation. One person may be only slightly affected by a demon, such as a spirit that causes occasional pain. Aside from pain, the host may exhibit no other symptoms of demonization. Other individuals may be severely affected by evil spirits. This is most common when multiple demons afflict a person with both emotional conditions like anxiety and fear and symptoms of physical illness.

Next, we'll discuss how demons are removed. The gospels of the New Testament reveal how Jesus and His disciples removed evil spirits and healed the sick. In the gospel of Luke, we read how Jesus empowered His disciples.

> *Then He called His twelve disciples together and gave them power and authority over all demons, and to cure diseases. He sent them to preach the kingdom of God and to heal the sick.*
> LUKE 9:1-2

Removing Evil Spirits

Jesus gave His disciples two things: power and authority. He did so to accomplish two purposes: Healing diseases and removing demons. The parallel passage in Matthew chapter 10 provides more details about what the disciples were supposed to do with their power and authority:

> *"And as you go, preach, saying, 'The kingdom of heaven is at hand.' Heal the sick, cleanse the lepers, raise the dead, cast out demons."*
> MATT. 10:7-8

Jesus instructed his disciples to raise the dead, cast out demons, and heal incurable diseases. Note that the Lord did not tell them to ask God for healing or deliverance. Instead, He gave His followers power and authority and instructed them to heal the sick themselves and remove demons. Power is released to work creative miracles. Authority is used to remove demons and cure diseases. (The use of power and authority for healing is discussed in my book, *Power and Authority Made Simple*.)

Although the authority needed to cast out demons comes from God, it is wielded by us. Let's look at an example of how evil spirits are removed:

> *Now it happened, as we went to prayer, that a certain slave girl possessed with a spirit of divination met us, who brought her masters much profit by fortune-telling. This girl followed Paul and us, and cried out, saying, "These men are the servants of the Most High God, who proclaim to us the way of salvation." And this she did for many days. But Paul, greatly annoyed, turned and said to the spirit, "I command you in the name of Jesus Christ to come out of her." And he came out that very hour.*
> ACTS 16:16-18

Although the slave girl correctly surmised that the disciples were servants of God, Paul discerned the presence of an evil spirit. Using his authority, he commanded the demon to leave, and it did. Let's look at an example of how Jesus removed a demon:

> *Now He was teaching in one of the synagogues on the Sabbath. And behold, there was a woman who had a spirit of infirmity eighteen years, and was bent over and could in no way raise herself up. But when Jesus saw her, He called her to Him and said to her, "Woman,*

EMOTIONAL HEALING AND DELIVERANCE MADE SIMPLE

you are loosed from your infirmity." And He laid His hands on her, and immediately she was made straight, and glorified God.
LUKE 13:10-13

In this passage, two things are worth noting: first, the woman was bound by a spirit of infirmity, which afflicted her physical body, causing her to be bent over. Jesus discerned the spirit's presence and exercised authority over it. In this case, He didn't confront the demon. He simply said, "You are set free from your infirmity," and the demon left. After the woman was freed from the demon, He laid His hands on her and healed her deformed body. She still needed physical healing after the spirit left because she was still bent over. We should not assume that physical healing has occurred because we've cast a demon out. After the spirit is removed, the person may still require physical healing.

In Luke 11, we find a discussion between Jesus and the religious leaders about the practice of casting out demons. We'll begin in verse 14, where we read about how Jesus cast out a spirit that caused a man to be mute.

And He was casting out a demon, and it was mute. So it was, when the demon had gone out, that the mute spoke; and the multitudes marveled. But some of them said, "He casts out demons by Beelzebub, the ruler of the demons."

Others, testing Him, sought from Him a sign from heaven. But He, knowing their thoughts, said to them: "Every kingdom divided against itself is brought to desolation, and a house divided against a house falls. If Satan also is divided against himself, how will his kingdom stand? Because you say I cast out demons by Beelzebub. And if I cast out demons by Beelzebub, by whom do your sons cast them out? Therefore, they will be your judges. But if I cast out demons with the finger of God, surely the kingdom of God has come upon you.
LUKE 11:14-20

Jesus explained that it was foolish to think one could cast out the servants of Satan (demons) by the authority of Satan. He then proposed that if He cast out demons by the finger of God, it was evidence that the kingdom of God had come.

Removing Evil Spirits

A demon will not always leave after a single command. And even if one does, it may return. Jesus explained using an allegory how and why demons sometimes return.

> *"When a strong man, fully armed, guards his own palace, his goods are in peace. But when a stronger than he comes upon him and overcomes him, he takes from him all his armor in which he trusted, and divides his spoils ....When an unclean spirit goes out of a man, he goes through dry places, seeking rest; and finding none, he says, 'I will return to my house from which I came.' And when he comes, he finds it swept and put in order. Then he goes and takes with him seven other spirits more wicked than himself, and they enter and dwell."*
> LUKE 11:21-22, 24-26

Jesus likened an evil spirit to a strongman who is armored and keeps his home. Note that demons see our bodies as their homes. He explained (metaphorically) that when one who is stronger comes, he removes the demon's armor, evicts him from the place he calls home, and divides his goods. The one who is stronger is a faith-filled believer. The "goods" He spoke of are the areas of a person's life that are held in bondage by the demon—typically physical illness and emotional trauma. He said that once removed, the demon may return to its home later if the dwelling remains intact.

How do we remove a demonic home?

Some teach that a person must be filled with the Holy Spirit to prevent a demon from returning. That idea isn't implied in this teaching, and I know many Spirit-filled believers who are attacked by demons. Jesus illustrated something else. Demons afflict us for specific reasons. There is a root cause for demonic attacks. If the root cause is not identified and remedied, the evil spirit may return and bring other demons with more afflictions. These demons manifest symptoms as diverse as chronic pain, autoimmune disease, panic attacks, and tumors. The battle against recurring illness and pain caused by demons is like the way in which we might deal with a criminal who repeatedly breaks into our home. Burglars are opportunistic. They size up their victims and evaluate their defenses, looking for signs of vulnerability. They look for alarm systems, unlocked doors and windows, the absence of a dog, and the likelihood that the homeowner will be unarmed. They look for homeowners that are unlikely to fight back. Demons do the same thing. They look for points of entry through emotional wounds that present as anger, shame, pride, fear, and other negative emotions. The best way to protect ourselves against demons is to remove the emotional wounds that allow them access to us. Before we address specific techniques, I'd like to examine the different types of demons we might encounter.

God's creativity is seen in all of nature. No two snowflakes are identical, and no two people are exactly alike. The same is true for demons. They are unique and have certain weaknesses, strengths, and abilities. Each demon is a specialist in one area and manifests its own brand of affliction. This differentiation was mentioned by Jesus.

And when they had come to the multitude, a man came to Him, kneeling down to Him and saying, "Lord, have mercy on my son, for he is an epileptic and suffers severely; for he often falls into the fire and often into the water. So I brought him to Your disciples, but they could not cure him."

Then Jesus answered and said, "O faithless and perverse generation, how long shall I be with you? How long shall I bear with you? Bring him here to Me." And Jesus rebuked the demon, and it came out of him; and the child was cured from that very hour.

Then the disciples came to Jesus privately and said, "Why could we not cast it out?"

So Jesus said to them, "Because of your unbelief; for assuredly, I say to you, if you have faith as a mustard seed, you will say to this mountain, 'Move from here to there,' and it will move; and nothing will be impossible for you. However, this kind does not go out except by prayer and fasting."
MATT 17:14-21

Jesus told the disciples that the demon did not come out because of their unbelief. The authority used to remove demons is activated by faith. Jesus said the *kind* of demon they encountered did not come out except by prayer and fasting. The implication was that there are different types of demons. The word that is translated as "kind" in this verse is the Greek word γένος (genos), from which we get the English word "genealogy." This word describes the differentiation between related varieties of living beings—specifically between families, races, tribes, or nations. Apparently, there are different families or races of demons, and the one they encountered was unique.

Some demons specialize in physical affliction, as with the woman who had been crippled by a spirit of infirmity for eighteen years. Other demons specialize in emotional trauma, like the spirit that terrorized King Saul with what might be diagnosed today as anxiety attacks (see 1 Sam 18:10). Some spirits specialize in divination, as was the case with the spirit the apostle Paul cast from the woman who followed him.

In each of these cases, the evil spirits did not exert complete control over the individual. Although King Saul suffered anxiety, he had no physical ailments. The woman who was physically crippled by a demon had no mental or emotional infirmity. The woman with the spirit of divination did not exhibit convulsions. Each of these individuals still retained their own identity and did not display signs of complete control by the evil spirit.

Demons frequently gain access to us through emotional trauma. Many emotional wounds occur during childhood. If one does not experience love, they have an unmet emotional need. For example, an unmet need to be loved can cause one to use pornography in an attempt to meet the emotional need. The unmet need serves as a home for evil spirits that specialize in lust, pornography, and sexual perversion. Knowing they have a home, demons take up residence in the person's soul.

The first step to removing the demon(s) is addressing the root cause, which in this case, is a lack of love. The individual must understand how much they are loved and accepted by their heavenly Father. The awareness of God's love destroys the unmet need for love and acceptance. The love of the Father destroys the demonic home. Once this is done, spirits of lust or pornography can be removed since their home has been destroyed.

EMOTIONAL HEALING AND DELIVERANCE MADE SIMPLE

In some cases, a traumatic event creates a soul wound. The wound causes us to feel negative emotions like anger, shame, or guilt. Jesus can heal these wounds. When they are healed, the emotions are removed, and the demonic home is destroyed. The following testimony demonstrates this principle.

> Around 7th or 8th grade, I, a late-blooming, prepubescent boy, was routinely sodomized by my brother, who was three years my senior. I really never considered this the source of my sexual immorality, pornography addiction, and general perversion until I was set free. I rarely thought of it later in life, but when I did, anger was the predominant emotion. I was angry when I was taken advantage of. I was also ashamed that I allowed myself to be taken advantage of.
>
> After reading Emotional Healing in 3 Easy Steps, I decided to try out the simple methods. I remember being skeptical that it could be so easy to get healed from a lifetime of anger and shame. Immediately after making a plea to Jesus to take this anger from me, I realized I had no desire to watch pornography. Soon thereafter, I continued with the emotional healing asking Jesus to take away my shame.
>
> It has been over a year and a half now, and I feel normal. I am able to talk with a woman and be around a woman without thinking about having sex with her. I am able to see her as a daughter of the most high and respect that, something that was always out of my reach for the previous 40 years. To this day, I am uncomfortable watching any sex or nude scenes in television shows or movies. I even look away at women's underwear commercials. I was able to forgive my brother after all these years but was unable to tell him in person as he had passed away a year prior. I believe now that these are normal reactions for normal people, and I am thankful to Jesus for setting me free, and I am thankful to Praying Medic for showing me how.

Deliverance Testimonies

Removing evil spirits can be a straightforward process. A demon is identified, and authority is exercised to remove it. The following testimony describes one such encounter:

> In 1980, my husband and I were married and baptized in the Holy Spirit on a Monday night in the back of a florist shop. The minister, a lady preacher who owned the shop, operated in the gifts of the spirit, and at that same ceremony, my maid of honor was

Removing Evil Spirits

delivered of several demons, and I experienced a miracle healing from a back injury that God revealed to the minister through a word of knowledge. We became part of a church that later had ministry teams that would minister inner healing and deliverance to people who requested prayer. I had a pastor who described me as "one of those who probably should have been locked up for the first two years after she was filled with the Holy Spirit." He was right. Once I experienced the reality of God's presence, the pursuit of His Spirit and His Word became the driving force in my life. I wanted (and still want) all of Him and I didn't want anything standing between me and anything He had for me. That was why I had requested prayer.

The two ladies who ministered to me were quite a team. Peggy was bold and vibrant. Edie was soft-spoken and carried a real anointing for the peace of God. The prayer began quietly. I stood there in front of them as we all prayed quietly in tongues. We were in the sanctuary, and there were several other ministry teams scattered around the room praying for people. We always had soft praise music in the background during these group sessions.

I remember Peggy prophesying to me, and as she ministered to me, Edie moved around to stand behind me and placed her hand on my back, to the right of my spine, between my shoulder blades. As I write this, I realize that was where I received healing for my spine at our wedding. For some reason, when intercessors pray for me, they tend to put their hands right there. (Thank you, Holy Ghost! I think that will come in handy for the full manifestation of healing I need now. Now, back to the deliverance testimony.)

Suddenly, the atmosphere shifted. Soft-spoken Edie became louder. "I recognize you, spirit of Fear! You will not hide! You are leaving her today," she said firmly, and with obvious authority.

Peggy agreed with her, saying, "Come out of her, Fear! In the Name of Jesus! You and all your dirty roots! Now!"

To my surprise, I heard a simpering voice inside of me that said, "But we've been with her so long…"

I didn't say those words. I just heard them inside of me. Apparently, Edie heard them, too, because she said loudly, "I don't care how long you've been with her or how many of you are there; you are coming out in Jesus' Name!" Peggy and Edie's voices got louder as they prayed in tongues, and even though I was aware they were getting louder, it seemed to me they were off in the distance somewhere. I felt like there was a giant corkscrew that went from my toes to the top of my head, and I could feel it slowly twisting its way out of me, turning, coming out the top of my head! I could still hear the ladies praying in tongues and English. They were in full warfare mode as that thing continued to turn and unravel right out of me. They kept praying. In my mind, I was transported to a time in my childhood when I was about five or six, and I was lying on a twin bed and felt smothered and paralyzed by Fear and darkness. At different times in my life, that smothering feeling would come over me. They weren't called panic attacks back then, but I am pretty sure that's what they would call them now.

I don't really remember much after that in the ministry session. One or both of them continued to talk to the spirit, telling it would not manifest or tear me as it left. I just remember that twisting corkscrew (which, over the years, I have come to think has something to do with my DNA) and the darkness and smothering feeling. I wound up on the floor covered with a prayer cloth, and the ladies continued to stand over me, walking around me and praying quietly in tongues. I think some other prayer ministers may have come over and joined in the fray, too. After it was over, someone brought me some water and told me to stay down until God was done ministering to me.

From that time on, although I experienced Fear from time to time, it was an external rather than an internal experience. Whatever tried to come upon me lost whatever it had inside me. I had read about and messed with some occult stuff when I was a child and teen, and a lot of that stuff left during that prayer session. I ended up ministering on the prayer and deliverance teams, too.

Deliverance from oppressive spirits may be done with the help of someone with experience, but it can also be done without assistance in some circumstances. The following testimony was submitted to me by a woman who worked through her own emotional healing and then commanded her own deliverance.

I have always struggled with this feeling of not belonging enough to just relax and enjoy life, ever since my mother left for medical reasons when I was four. Doing the emotional healing, it started to dawn on me that this kind of depressed, never really "home" feeling is demonic in nature, and it has gotten worse.

I went through the emotional healing steps for when my mother left, and it helped. But since then, thoughts I do not recognize and would not ever think started trying to creep in. Last night, a fleeting thought of blowing my head off flitted across my mind. It was 3 am, and I immediately started rebuking this spirit of depression and telling

Removing Evil Spirits

it I know I have the authority and power to command it to leave. (Being a recovering Catholic, this is a new concept.)

I started shivering and feeling sick to my stomach, but I kept on rebuking, demanding, and standing on my authority. It tried to tell me only priests were given the authority. I called on Jesus and told him my body is His alone, and I reject this depression that is trying to take over.

I was shaking and shivering and so cold and sick to my stomach, but I did not give up. I felt like I was going to throw up, so I ran into the bathroom and continued to demand this spirit of depression leave now, now, now, and it has no choice!

I was commanding out loud and speaking the name of Jesus, and suddenly I sounded like a demon! It was trying to stop me. I was saying that I was commanding it in the name of Jesus Chri...

It choked me from finishing saying it! So again, I said it very loudly, my body is the temple of Jesus Christ!

I threw up some white weird looking stuff three times. Then, I made three big burps. I was still shaking and shivering. My temp had climbed to 100 degrees.

I went back under the covers and shivered for another hour. By the time I felt warm again, it was 7 am.

Those who experience deliverance from evil spirits may report feeling strange bodily sensations during the process. The most common are yawing, retching, vomiting, and belching. Less common are muscle tremors, twitching, and involuntary arm or leg movements. Sometimes, the individual will experience increased pain.

Deliverance from evil spirits can be a simple process, but sometimes, it's quite an ordeal. Testimonies like the one above might make you think it isn't worth the time and discomfort. God knows the most effective way to set you free from evil spirits. He will not ask you to submit to a long, difficult process if it is not necessary.

CHAPTER FOURTEEN

Emotional Healing of Back Pain

IT SEEMS COUNTERINTUITIVE TO IMAGINE that chronic back pain might be caused by an emotional wound that created a home for a demon. This is the true story of my encounter with a woman who was healed of back pain after receiving emotional healing.

A few years ago, my wife Denise and I stayed at a hotel near Tacoma, Washington, where a conference was being held on supernatural healing. As Denise and I checked in to the hotel, we talked with a woman behind the desk named Susan. I told her we were the featured speakers for the conference and gave her some background information about us. Susan said she attended a Charismatic church and wanted to know more about healing. I was tired from the trip and wanted to get to our room and unpack our bags, so I pulled out a copy of my book, *Divine Healing Made Simple*, from my bag, autographed it, and handed it to Susan. "We'll be here for nine days," I said. "We'd be more than happy to answer any questions you have." She thanked us, and we went to our room.

The following day, I received a message from a woman named Emily, who works at the hotel registration desk at night. She found Susan's copy of the book and began reading it. When she was halfway through the book, she contacted me through Facebook. She had been suffering from chronic back pain from four different car accidents and asked about emotional healing. We set up a meeting at the home of a friend.

When Emily arrived for her appointment, we spent a few minutes getting to know her. She had been feeling anxiety that morning. When I asked how her back pain was, she said, "My back feels like it's on fire." The pain was so bad she considered turning around, driving home, and skipping the appointment. When you make an appointment for healing or deliverance, it is not unusual to feel fear, anxiety, or an increase in the symptoms you want to be healed of as the appointment time draws near. Evil spirits are aware of our thoughts. As the time of healing and deliverance draws near, they know their time is short, and they frequently manifest as increased fear, anxiety, and pain just before or during the healing encounter. Their goal is to frighten their host, hoping to get them to cancel the appointment. Emily sat on a couch and agreed to have me pray with her. I began by asking Emily if she had been abused either sexually, physically, or verbally as a child. I started with this question because it seems to be the most common cause of emotional wounds. Emily said she had been verbally and physically abused by her father. I asked if she could recall a specific event from her past that evoked a strong negative emotion. She recalled a birthday from her childhood when her father promised to take her out for dinner. That night he went to a bar and got drunk, and forgot about her. When he came home, she asked if he would take her out for her birthday. He grudgingly agreed to take her to McDonald's, but as she walked to the car, he kicked her all the way to the car. "So when you recall your father kicking you, what emotion comes to mind?"

"Worthlessness," she replied.

I said, "Emily, I want you to repeat after me. Jesus, I ask you to take this feeling of worthlessness from me." She repeated what I said. "I don't

Emotional Healing of Back Pain

want it anymore. I ask you to heal the wound in my soul caused by it." Again, she repeated what I said. "In place of worthlessness, I ask you to give me honor." She repeated my words again. "Jesus, I receive your healing." She repeated this, and when she was done, I had her recall the event with her father again.

"So there you are, waiting for your father to come home. He gets there, and you ask if he'll take you out for dinner. You're on your way to the car, and he's kicking you. What emotion do you feel?"

"I guess... it's just disappointment."

"Okay, we're going to do the same thing for disappointment. Repeat after me. Jesus, I ask you to take the feeling of disappointment from me. I don't want it anymore. I ask you to heal the wound in my soul caused by it. In place of disappointment, I ask you to give me hope. Jesus, I receive your healing." When she had said these words, I asked her again to recall the event with her father and tell me what emotion she felt.

"Fear."

"Okay, we're going to do the same thing with fear. Repeat after me. Jesus, I ask you to take the feeling of fear from me. I don't want it anymore. I ask you to heal the wound in my soul caused by it. In place of fear, I ask you to give me courage. Jesus, I receive your healing." When she finished saying the words, I asked her again to recall the event with her father and tell me what emotion she felt.

She paused for a moment and finally said, "Nothing. I can remember it all, but there aren't any emotions I can really feel."

"Cool. That means you're healed of the wounds in your soul from that event. Let's move on to the next one. You said you had been married twice. Did either of your ex-husbands abuse you?"

"Yes. They both did."

"What kind of abuse was it? Did they physically hit you, or was it verbal abuse?"

"Both my ex-husbands hit me, and we got into a lot of arguments."

"Okay. We're going to do the same thing. Is there one event with your most recent ex-husband that causes you to feel a strong negative emotion?" She told me about how they would argue, and her ex-husband would punch her in the face to end the argument. "Okay, Emily, so there you are with your husband, and you get into another argument. It escalates into a yelling match, and he punches you in the face. Tell me what emotion you're feeling."

"Anger," she replied as tears streamed down her cheeks.

"Okay, we're going to do the same thing with anger that we did with the other emotions. Repeat after me. Jesus, I ask you to take the feeling of anger from me. I don't want it anymore. I ask you to heal the wound in my soul caused by it. In place of anger, I ask you to give me peace. Jesus, I receive your healing." When she was finished saying the words, I had her take a short break because she was crying. After she regained her composure, I asked her again to recall the argument with her ex-husband and tell me what emotion she felt.

"Hurt. That's the only way I can describe it."

"Okay. We'll go with that. Are you ready?"

"Yes, I'm ready."

"Jesus, I ask you to take the feeling of hurt from me. I don't want it anymore. I ask you to heal the wound in my soul caused by it. In place of hurt, I ask you to give me healing. Jesus, I receive your healing." She repeated each sentence. When she was done, we went back to the same event. "Okay, Emily, so there you are with your husband, and you get into another argument, and he punches you in the face. Tell me what emotion you're feeling."

"Fear."

"Okay. You're doing great. Take a breath. We're going to get rid of fear whenever you're ready."

"I'm ready."

"Repeat after me. Jesus, I ask you to take the feeling of fear from me. I don't want it anymore. I ask you to heal the wound in my soul caused by it. In place of fear, I ask you to give me confidence. Jesus, I receive your healing." When she was done, I had her recall the argument one more time. "What emotion do you feel?"

"I'm not really feeling anything this time."

"Awesome. So those emotional wounds are healed. Thank you Jesus! Let's move on to your first husband. Is there any event from your first marriage that causes strong negative emotions?"

She told me about an event that caused similar feelings to those she had when she got into a fight with her second husband. We followed the same steps as before. She identified each emotion and asked Jesus to heal them. We then went back into the memory of the event to see what emotions were left until all the negative emotions were gone.

"I have a question for you, Emily. How does your back feel right now?"

"It feels really good," she said with a beaming smile. "It was really bad when I got here, but now there's just a little pain right here," she said, pointing to a spot on the right side in the middle of her back.

"Now that we've removed the emotional wounds the spirit used to afflict you, it should be easy to heal the pain you still have." I had her stand up. I commanded her back to be healed, and the pain immediately left.

I gave her a short lesson on why back pain from a car accident would require emotional healing, which I'll summarize:

Evil spirits are opportunistic, like most predators. Predators take advantage of weakness because weakness gives them an advantage. A shark becomes aggressive when it smells blood in the water. Vultures gather around dying animals. Demons flock to people who are suffering trauma, both physical and emotional, because trauma weakens us physically and emotionally. When Emily had her car accident, she may have suffered physiological damage to her body, but she also suffered emotional damage to her soul. It's likely that an evil spirit attached itself to her soul at the time of the accident—either to a new emotional wound or one that had existed previously. As time passed and her physical injuries healed, the pain in her back remained because the emotional wound was still there, providing a home for a spirit of pain. Unlike physical wounds that heal over time, emotional wounds remain in our souls until Jesus heals them. As long as an emotional wound remains intact, the symptoms caused by the spirit attached to the wound will not leave. The only way to remove the symptoms is to heal the emotional wound.

CHAPTER FIFTEEN

Emotional Roots of Physical Illness

AS THE PREVIOUS CHAPTER DEMONSTRATES, many illnesses or injuries that appear to be physiological are rooted in emotional trauma. As we age, unhealed emotional wounds often manifest as illness and chronic pain. When emotional trauma is healed, the symptoms resolve. In the following testimony, Dena Grace shares her healing story:

> In January 2022, a friend of mine was supernaturally healed of celiac disease. It occurred after a Saturday night worship service. One of the guest speakers was still on stage, surrounded by children, and pointed to the area where my friend was standing. They said, "I feel someone over here has been dealing with chronic, severe celiac. God wants to heal you. Who is it?"
>
> Before my friend could fully raise his hand, he was flung sideways by the Spirit. He lay on the floor shaking for a long time. His wife helped him home. The next morning, he held a cracker in his hands. He had no blistering of the skin, no rash, no reaction.

EMOTIONAL HEALING AND DELIVERANCE MADE SIMPLE

He was tested, and the results showed that celiac was gone! No human touched him.

Encouraged by his testimony, I started to go after my own chronic issues centered in my gut and ankle. For ten years, I've been plagued with intestinal discomfort, irritability, and other issues. I had exhausted all western medicine regimens, had wearied my naturopath, had tried acupuncture, herbs, chiropractics, you name it. Appeasement would come for short periods, but, bam! Every November, they flooded back full strength.

This year, November arrived with symptoms surging out of nowhere. I cried out: "God! What is going on? I need relief. Help me, please!" I felt led to visit a local healing room. Nothing happened, but one of the ministers asked me, "What happened around the time this started? I feel your gut issues have an emotional root."

Blankly, I stared at her. I couldn't remember... but God did. And He reminded me the next morning.

It was November 2012, right before Thanksgiving, a time when I experienced intense rejection, betrayal, and humiliation that I was unable to deal with in the moment. I had to put it aside for when I was home, and I was able to process it.

Later that day, I listened to an interview, and a comment caught my ear "90 plus percent of all chronic illness has an emotional root."

I thought it was an overstatement until God asked: "What did you do with all the feelings, emotions, and judgments you had, Dena?"

"I swallowed them," I replied.

A long, holy, pause. "And that is where they have remained."

An astonished, lights going on, acknowledgment and agreement moment occurred. I immediately went into repentance and forgiveness mode. I repented for partnering, sheltering, giving home to rejection, betrayal, humiliation, to the harmful, to the twisted. I kicked them out. I told them to leave. I forgave all parties (again). Cut all ties (again). Repented of all judgments (again). I felt better; my symptoms improved 70 percent with one prayer. Hallelujah, Praise Jesus!

But 70 percent is not 100 percent. I wanted complete healing, not partial, not kinda, not sorta, or a bit. I wanted all. I continued to press God for more, and felt led to call my pastor, who has a heart for deliverance. A week later, I was in his office. We went to work. In thirty minutes, snotty and tear-stained, I left his office 100 percent symptom free! I have been ever since. No acid reflux. No bloating. No abdominal pain. No indigestion. No cramping. And I'm able to ingest dairy, gluten, sugar, caffeine, steak, soy, oats…All. The. Things! Believe me, I have Tested this! Again, Hallelujah, Praise Jesus!

"The testimony of Jesus is the Spirit of prophecy." Rev. 19:10.

My friend's testimony provoked my healing; hopefully, mine can inspire yours.

NOTE - *Dena's testimony was first published on her website here: https://www.denagrace.com/post/i-swallowed-it*

CHAPTER SIXTEEN

Healed of Alcoholism

MANY FORMS OF ADDICTION ARE rooted in unhealed emotional trauma. When emotional wounds are healed, the spirits of addiction can be removed, and the individual loses their addictive craving. Brian Fenimore is a gifted teacher and friend. We've posted several of our live stream broadcasts on my Rumble channel. In one broadcast, we discussed deliverance from evil spirits. The following testimony is from a woman named Cynthia, who was set free of alcoholism after watching that video.

> I have been meaning to sit down and write this since you started focusing primarily on healing again through Telegram. The Brian Fenimore videos and your video healing prayers have helped me so much, especially the emotional healing. I asked you on Telegram if you thought it was possible to cure alcoholism. You stated that it is, and that emotional healing would be the best place to start. Well, I have had many of your books for a long time, including Emotional Healing. My problem is: I buy books with an addictive personality, too. I get them, read the introduction and first chapter or two,

then move on to the next squirrel that gets my attention. I go through cycles of intense spiritual healing and communication with Spirit and then shut down and just want to avoid the next layer for a while.

Revisiting the Emotional Healing book, it just clicked this time because I had such a profound experience listening to the Brian Fenimore videos with you. When you both prayed for listeners, I literally fell to my knees in tears and could feel the Lord working on deep, deep layers of issues I had buried for a long time.

When I started on the emotional healing steps and asked the Holy Spirit to show me what He wanted me to heal, it was like a floodgate of memories and emotions started revealing themselves to me. Some issues I was able to take one memory and emotion at a time, while Jesus showed me that others, which repeated themselves over and over in my life (especially shameful episodes related to my alcoholism) could be grouped and healed at one time. The Lord showed me such tenderness and beautiful visions. I just want to say that I have no desire to drink. I also worked through many other emotions related to relationships and my perception of myself.

For physical healing, the concept of demonic attachment and oppression being a primary cause has been revolutionary in how I approach my health and healing. I've always been into natural healing and taking care of myself, despite the alcoholism. More of an all-or-nothing cycle of self-sabotage. Now, if any kind of aches, pains, and/or negative thinking begins to bring me down, this is the first line of defense I go to.

Your healing prayers are invaluable! In the beginning, I was listening every night to one of the three main ones, especially the nervous system healing prayer. Now, if I can't sleep, the prayers and your healing voice calm me and lull me to sleep. They've also helped in my own meditative healing prayers because of the specific structure and technique you use.

Anyway, I could go on and on. One of the reasons it's taken me so long to do this. Too much to say in a pithy Telegram or Truth Social post. Thank you! Thank you! Thank you! God bless you and Denise and your ministry. You are helping so many people on such a deep level.

Love and Light,
Cynthia

CHAPTER SEVENTEEN

Healing Through Worship

DEVELOPING INTIMACY WITH GOD IS a powerful way to receive healing. In addition to daily conversations, we can express our love for God through worship. We sometimes forget that worship is a form of spiritual warfare. As the following testimony demonstrates, worship can bring healing of physical illness and emotional trauma.

> Hey PM, a little update. I told you a couple of days ago that I felt like God wants my worship and a closer relationship with Him. To come and sit before Him without expectations, just enjoy Him. I put aside my phone and stopped checking for the latest news. Used that time instead to pray. I quit listening to the prophets I usually tune into because I felt like God wanted me to hear from Him directly.
>
> I began to pray while going about my house work and in between interactions with my family. Basically a running commentary. Something I used to do all the time before getting a smart phone.

I was sitting in my chair yesterday morning, struggling with pain. I have TMJ (my jaw pops out), and it hurts. I have sinus infections, headaches, and my eyeballs hurt. I usually go to the chiropractor to have him pop it back in, but I was JUST there and didn't want to spend the $50.

I began to worship. I felt like Holy Spirit told me to ask for healing. I did, and the pain began to drain from the top of my head down. It was intense warfare. My pain was pretty significant, and it kept trying to come back. God told me that there were five spirits of pain. As I cast each one out, my pain lessened. My ears began popping! Anyway, long story short, my pain is almost completely gone. I believe God told me that it was a stronghold of pain and other things like shame, self-hatred, and a few other things. He showed me when the stronghold was set up. I'm still praying about this because I believe that I can be 100% healed, and if I allow even a little discomfort to stay, it will come back worse.

But I guess the biggest eye-opening thing to me is how powerful worship is. I knew it, but I'd forgotten the raw power and comfort that comes when we choose to worship and sit attentively at His feet. I had several words from Him and direction about how to get further emotional healing.

There is some warfare happening in my family because I've chosen to do this. Our dog got hit and killed, my hubby's blood pressure is bothering him, and my daughter had some stomach issues. All just out of the blue in one day. But I'm not going to relent. I want more Jesus!

Healing and deliverance are ways in which we conduct spiritual warfare. Warfare implies the existence of an enemy. When you endeavor to set yourself and others free of sickness or demons, you are stepping onto the field of battle and you should expect retaliation. Fear is a common tactic of the enemy. You may also experience new or more severe symptoms. Do not submit to fear. Ask God for strategies to overcome the attacks.

CHAPTER EIGHTEEN

The Spiritual Senses

ALTERS, FRAGMENTS, ANGELS, AND DEMONS are invisible to the naked eye. If we are to perceive them and their actions and hope to communicate with them, it must be done through our spiritual senses. Our ability to facilitate emotional healing and deliverance depends on sensing what is happening in the spiritual world. While it isn't absolutely necessary to see in the spirit or hear God's voice, these abilities make the process easier and more effective.

Those who operate in emotional healing are typically aided by their spiritual vision. They can usually see a representation of an alter or fragment. The appearance of an alter and the environment in which it lives provide clues to the nature of the problems that must be addressed. Similarly, the appearance of a demon and its actions that we observe provide information that can be used to evict it. If we want to see alters and demons, we must develop our spiritual eyesight.

EMOTIONAL HEALING AND DELIVERANCE MADE SIMPLE

Seeing in the spiritual world is not a special gift only given to a few people. It is an innate ability we all possess that can be developed through exercise. The same is true of our ability to hear spiritual beings. Humans are, first and foremost, created as spirits. We are a spirit. We have a soul, and we inhabit a physical body. Our spiritual body has all the senses of the physical body save for one difference: our spirit can communicate telepathically through the transmission of thoughts.

If a demon spoke to a woman sitting next to you in a restaurant, you would not hear what the demon said, but the woman would. Likewise, if God were to speak to her, you would not hear what was said. Spirit beings can direct their messages to specific people while concealing them from those who are nearby. They can also manifest their appearance to specific individuals while remaining invisible to others. This is why some people see demons and angels while those nearby see nothing.

Some of us have difficulty seeing the spiritual world. If we are a spirit that is created with spiritual eyes that can see in the spiritual world, then the problem isn't that we don't have the visual apparatus to do it, or that we lack the proper anointing or spiritual gift. The problem is that our soul has not been conditioned to correctly perceive what our spiritual eyes already observe.

Our spirit perceives beings in the spiritual world continuously, even if we are unaware of them. Images seen by our spiritual eyes are conveyed to our soul and displayed on an apparatus in our mind called our imagination (or the mind's eye). Communication by spiritual beings is usually done through the transmission of thoughts. When the Spirit of God speaks to us, it is usually perceived as a barely perceptible thought impression. Some refer to this phenomenon as the "still, small voice" of God. Angels, demons, and wounded parts of the soul speak in the same way.

God's voice is external to us, but His Spirit resides in us. Thus, when He speaks, we perceive His external voice as an internal experience. We perceive His thoughts as our own thoughts. The way in which God's thoughts come to us is so subtle it's often hard to recognize that they have their origin outside of us. The Bible says that His ways are not our ways, and His thoughts are not our thoughts. The thoughts

He shares with us are different from our own. The brilliant, inspired, loving, compassionate thoughts that come to mind at seemingly random times are the thoughts of God spoken to us by the His Spirit. The same is true for visual images that we receive. Many times, we will think an image in our mind came from our imagination when in fact, it came from God. Half the battle of knowing that what you're seeing, feeling, or hearing is from God is simply knowing that it isn't from you.

It's natural to wonder if something we saw or heard originated in our own mind or the mind of God. For some, there is too much uncertainty over knowing the origin of an idea that they prefer not to attempt to discern what God might be saying for fear of being wrong. Determining the origin of revelation may seem daunting, but we can take a few simple steps to verify the source of any revelation.

God can speak to us through visions, dreams, aromas, emotions, skin sensations, and thought impressions that carry messages to our mind. It's common to attribute these things to an over-active imagination. But there are ways we can distinguish God's voice from our own thoughts.

The believer has their own spirit and the Spirit of God living in them. These two spirits are the sources of two different kinds of thought or streams of revelation. Before we can know which thoughts are God's, we must first know which belong to us. One problem many of us have is that we do not know our own thoughts the way we should. When we know ourselves well and clearly understand how our mind works, we can view our thoughts like an objective observer. The better we know our thoughts, the easier it is to discern the thoughts that are not ours, but God's. This technique also helps us identify the thoughts of alters and fragments. The first step in learning to distinguish our thoughts from God's is becoming more aware of the nature of our own thought life.

How do we know if a thought is from God or from another source?

Let's first see if we can determine whether a thought is internal to us or external. This issue is best explained with an illustration:

Imagine for a moment that you're the radio operator on board a ship at sea. Now imagine that your boat needs to communicate with another ship. Communication between ships is done by sending radio signals back and forth. As the radio operator on one ship, you might wonder how you can distinguish between the signals you send and those sent by another ship. Consider this fact: As the radio operator on your ship, you can control the content of the messages you send. You cannot control the messages coming from the other vessel. The fact that you cannot change a message coming from another ship means that the message had its origin somewhere else. The fact that you can change a message coming from your ship means that it originated on your ship. This same principle applies to messages from God, angels, demons, alters, and our soul.

Our soul creates its own messages, including thoughts, impressions, emotions, and visual images. One difference between the ones that come from an external source and ones that come from our soul is that those which come from an external source are impossible to manipulate or change willfully. Just like the radio message sent by another ship, a message that is external to us cannot be changed by us. In contrast, a message that originates in our soul can be changed by exerting our will over it.

A second principle to consider is that a message we might send to another ship requires our input. We must think of what we want to say and initiate the message willfully. Messages we receive from another ship are received passively, with no effort on our part. In the same way, images and messages we receive from external sources tend to appear spontaneously with no effort on our part or involvement of our will. Whereas messages that originate in our soul require some intention (we must exercise our will) to make them appear or disappear.

A third principle to consider is the fruit produced by what we hear. The Holy Spirit is called the Comforter, the Spirit of Grace, the Spirit of Peace, the Spirit of Wisdom, and the Spirit of Truth. These are the attributes (fruit) produced by God's revelation. If anyone hears the words of the Spirit and acts upon them, the same fruit will be produced in their life. The voice of the Spirit produces the fruit of the Spirit, which is love, joy, peace, longsuffering, kindness, goodness, faithfulness, gentleness, and self-control (Gal 5:22). If one says they are hearing from God, and they act upon what they have heard, but the fruit produced

The Spiritual Senses

is condemnation, fear, discord or any other negative quality, we can tell that this person was not hearing from God.

In addition to images of angels, demons, and alters—information we may need for healing or deliverance—the imagination displays the grotesque, the perverted, and the frightening images we've been exposed to over our lives. Because some of the imagery displayed in this part of the mind can be frightening or painful, to avoid pain or terror, some have exercised their will and chosen to shut down their imagination. In an attempt to safeguard their soul, they unknowingly blinded themselves spiritually. If you have difficulty seeing in the spiritual world, it could be that you've exercised your will and closed your mind off to the spiritual world. Sometimes, alters are exposed to grotesque images and tricked by demons into shutting down the imagination. If you were to exercise your will and make the conscious choice to receive revelation again through your imagination, your spiritual eyes will again be open, and you'll be able to see in the spirit. If the decision were made by an alter, you would need to explain the situation to them and ask them to open themselves to receiving revelation again. Many people sense the presence of an alter as another voice inside of them that thinks differently and expresses these differences in divergent thoughts. If you can identify such a voice, open a dialogue with them and ask them to relinquish control over your imagination. (You can speak these words aloud, or have the conversation in your mind with the alter.) The solution to seeing unpleasant things is not to avoid seeing everything that comes through our imagination, but learning to filter it by sanctifying our imagination for God's purposes.

I usually pray for others from the visions God shows me in my mind. As I pray, the vision usually changes according to the effects of my prayer. Let's illustrate what this looks like, practically.

Many alters are reluctant to meet Jesus because demons have deceived them into thinking the Lord is cruel. A typical lie told by a demon is that Jesus doesn't care about the alter. If He did, he would have prevented them from being abused. The truth is: God does not directly prevent abuse because it would require violating the free will of the abuser, and God will never negate free will. If I were praying for an alter who is deceived by a demon, I might issue an authoritative command that the demon is to be bound in chains and forced to remain silent. I would expect to see in my mind the demon bound in chains lying at the feet of the alter. (This is an effective tactic when dealing with alters that are deceived by demons.) I would then explain to the alter that Jesus cannot violate our free will and that He chose to be with them during the event rather than prevent their abuse directly. If the demon were not restrained, I would expect an argument from the alter, but when demonic interference is removed, an alter may agree to meet Jesus. If they did, I would expect to see a scene where the Lord is holding and comforting the alter during the traumatic event.

This dynamic does not require you to be in the room with the one you're assisting. I receive many prayer requests by e-mail from people around the world. When I receive a prayer request, I close my eyes and look to see what God wants to show me. Sometimes, I see the person I'm praying for standing or sitting in front of me in a vision, and I'll see a glowing ball of light begin to travel around inside their body. One day, I prayed this way for a man in Africa who had malaria. He reported the next day that his symptoms had disappeared overnight. I use this method of prayer nearly every day.

CHAPTER NINETEEN 19

The Other Me

ONE RESULT OF STUDYING DREAMS and emotional healing is the realization that God gives us clues to emotional healing through dreams. Many people have learned they have child alters after seeing them in dreams. Sometimes, a child appearing in a dream is unfamiliar to the dreamer. In other cases, the dreamer knows the child is a younger version of themselves. After realizing their dream was a hint that they needed emotional healing, many of them are living in greater freedom.

After my first emotional healing session with Matt Evans, we knew I needed more healing. My goal in the second session (which I didn't share with Matt) was to find a particular alter. So, we scheduled a second session.

Matt started like he usually does, asking the Holy Spirit to reveal various things about me. God revealed to him secrets that only a few people knew, like the fact that I don't let people get too close to me out of fear of what they might think once they know the truth about me. And that despite being an extrovert, I prefer long periods of seclusion. There were other things revealed as well. Everything that God showed Matt hinted at the existence of another me—a Mister Hyde to my Doctor Jekyll—a persona unknown to me, except through occasional, unexplained mood swings and a dream.

In the dream, there were two versions of me. One "me" was outgoing. He loved to socialize. The other "me" was a cave-dweller who wanted to be left alone. In the dream, the outgoing me counseled the cave-dwelling me and tried to convince him it was safe to come out of his cave. I told Matt about the dream. He took it as a sign that I may have a major alter.

I have no history of severe emotional trauma or the type of dissociation seen with dissociative identity disorder. But emotional trauma and dissociation occur on a spectrum. Most people suffer emotional trauma to one degree or another, which leads to the creation of fragments and alters. We all experience dissociation to greater or lesser degrees.

As Matt asked questions, I told him what I saw in my mind. I felt led to explore a wilderness area, and before long, I located the alter. He was living in an underground cavern somewhere inside of me. The cavern was long, with many adjacent chambers.

The usual method of healing an alter is to have them meet with Jesus. So, Matt asked Jesus to find my alter. In my mind, I saw Jesus standing in the cave beside the alter. The alter expressed a concern. (I sensed the expression of his concern as a thought in my mind.) While the concern was not something that I felt strongly about at the time, it is one that I've expressed at various times throughout my life, mostly when I'm under pressure to conform to people's expectations. The concern is that no one understands me. So, the alter asked Jesus if He understood him. (Again, I perceived this question as a thought in my mind.) Jesus said He did understand the alter. Then, the alter asked Jesus if he could be trusted. Jesus answered that He could be trusted. When the alter was satisfied with the answers, he went with Jesus. They came out of the cave and immediately went into heaven. I saw the trip to heaven from the alter's perspective. The view was spectacular. It was as if I was strapped to a rocket being sent into space. The sensation of peace and freedom I felt was incredible.

We found two other alters that were toddlers. They were sitting with Jesus in what looked like the living room of the house I had lived in 50 years earlier. We said some healing prayers for them, and they went with Jesus to a place in heaven.

Then, we found a group of fragments. They appeared as tiny soldiers scatted over a vast parcel of land that resembled a battlefield. In our previous session, we'd found many such fragments, which were healed and integrated. As before, we prayed for their healing and integration. I'd like to point out that in all these experiences with groups of fragments, we asked Jesus to heal the fragments first, and their clothing turned white. As a rule, I do not recommend integrating alters or fragments until they have been healed. One indication of healing is a change in the color of their clothing to white, which symbolizes purity.

When the healing session was over, I felt physically tired. But emotionally, I felt great.

The week after I was healed, I taught four nights in a row at a school of supernatural ministry. Although I enjoy teaching, I've always felt low-level fear and apprehension when in the spotlight. After teaching and praying with people in public, I usually feel emotionally drained and grumpy. I want to be left alone. So, I typically retire to the safety of my cave for a couple of weeks. Sometimes the seclusion lasts for months. Consecutive days of public speaking have always been difficult. But the week after I was healed, everything was different. After four nights of teaching, instead of feeling like I wanted to crawl in a cave, I felt energized. There was no resentment over the time I'd spent in public. I had no fear over what people might think of me. There were no worries about being misunderstood. I felt very normal. More normal than I had felt in decades.

If you feel like there are multiple people inside of you, there is hope. Jesus can heal and integrate the alters and fragments and help you live a more balanced, normal life.

EMOTIONAL HEALING AND DELIVERANCE MADE SIMPLE

If you're looking for another resource on this subject, Matt Evans and Diane Moyer have written a book titled, *Divine Healing for Spirit, Soul & Body.*

CHAPTER TWENTY

Interacting in the Spirit

THINGS THAT YOU SEE IN the spirit can take on different appearances from one moment to the next. You might see a tall, ferocious-looking demon confronting you one minute, but after you rebuke the spirit, it may change form and resemble a harmless cloud of dust. Angels can take on different appearances, manifesting as translucent beings of light or ordinary men and women.

People with well-developed spiritual vision sometimes see swords and spears impaled in others. They may see people or alters tied up in chains and other devices of torture. A prophetic act to remove the device, along with prayer for the affected person or alter will often bring freedom.

Tools, devices, castles, mountains, rivers, dragons, torture chambers, pyramids, angels, demons, or anything else you might see in the spirit have a real entity associated with them. While the image you see may not perfectly represent the object or being you're dealing with, the being or object it represents will respond to whatever you do to or with it in the spirit.

Thoughts and words in the spirit world are creative in nature. They are composed of the spiritual light of eternity that originates in the glory of God. When we speak of creative thought, we're not speaking of the "creative visualization" used by Buddhists and New Age practitioners, nor are we referring to the "positive thinking" that has been promoted by self-help gurus to imagine the circumstances they desire. We're talking about the kingdom of heaven empowering the human spirit to manifest the realities of heaven in both the physical and spiritual realms. I have better success healing a broken bone if I first visualize the bone being healed in my mind. Once I see it as it should be, I declare that it will be so in the physical realm. A prophetic act done in faith can create a reality in the spiritual world that has an effect in the physical world. Faith carries more weight than we realize. It's the currency of heaven that purchases—and in some cases creates—the realities we experience in the physical world.

Steve Harmon found a brilliant way to put this principle into practice. One day, he was ministering healing to a person with dissociative identity disorder. He had been working with them for some time and was teaching an alter about God. During these encounters, Steve will ask Jesus to assist in the process. The session was nearing an end, and the alter wanted to know what he should do until their next session. Steve asked Jesus for advice. Jesus told him to create a book about God for the alter to read. Steve asked Jesus, "How do I do that?" Jesus told him to speak it into existence. Using his imagination, Steve spoke into existence a spiritual book about God, then handed it to the alter and told him to read it. When they met during the next session, the alter told Steve the things he had learned about God by reading the book.

Most people who are accustomed to living by the laws of the physical world do not understand how an "imaginary" tool can be used to remove an "imaginary" shackle on an alter's wrist. Equally puzzling is when a short healing prayer combined with a prophetic act to remove an "imaginary" spear brings relief to someone's pain. The fact that something is not visible in the physical world does not mean it is not real. The words "invisible" and "imaginary" do not mean the same thing. Angels and demons are not usually visible in the physical world, but they are just as real as you or me. Paul wrote to believers in Corinth:

> *We do not look at the things which are seen, but at the things which are not seen. For the things which are seen are temporary, but the things which are not seen are eternal.*
> 2 COR. 4:18

There are structures inside the human soul that alters are familiar with, which serve as dwelling places for them. These places can be castles, hospitals, mansions, dungeons, cages, fields, streams, woods, planets, or almost any setting you can think of. There are also places that lie outside of the soul, but still in the spiritual world that can be seen by alters. Alters are extremely aware of the presence of angels and demons, though due to demonic lies, they're often confused about their real identities. The ministry of inner healing and deliverance must take into account the reality of these inner worlds that are invisible to our physical eyes. Seeing in the spirit can be of great benefit to anyone who hopes to minister to people who have these conditions.

In her ground-breaking book *Regions of Captivity*, Ana Mendez Ferrell describes her discovery of the fragmented souls of people who suffer severe abuse and neglect. Alters and fragments are often confined to prisons in various spiritual regions where they are abused and tormented by demons. She teaches an approach to rescuing them that involves seeing into these dark places, going there to open the prison gates, and releasing the captives. This process is usually done with the help of Jesus and angels who lead the way, deal with demon guards, and help unlock the prison doors. If God has called you to operate in a ministry such as this, it may require you to develop your ability to see what is happening in the spiritual world. Going into these unseen regions is one strategy that God is using to help free people from the power of darkness.

There is an odd yet beautiful reality of the inner world that is worth paying attention to. The general condition of the soul is often reflected in the appearance of the inner world. When a system is under severe demonic attack, the weather of the inner world may appear stormy and other elements appear to be in distress. When alters experience the goodness of God, the weather may be sunny, and rivers will flow with sparkling, clean water. If you are the one assisting with healing, the condition of the inner world and relevant alters may be revealed to you in visions. More often, the one who is receiving healing will see alters and aspects of the inner world in their mind. In the following testimony, Jesus healed the child alters in one woman's system, and we're given a glimpse at how it changed the appearance of her inner world.

> For over 40 years, I had been a Christian without ever feeling the love of God in my heart. I believed in His love; I could even hear the Father tell me that He loved me, but I couldn't feel it. Romans 5:5 with its statement that God had poured out His love into my heart, seemed a mockery. If that was normal, why then did the Bible also say that His perfect love cast out fear? My faith in His love sure didn't alleviate my fears.
>
> I knew Jesus was working in my heart. One time, many years ago, He had asked me, "May I touch your heart?" I was moved to tears at the time not only by His gentleness, but that He didn't just barge in and do what He wanted. This had been my experience with everybody else. Jesus, however, asked my permission. He respected my free will.
>
> Over the years, Jesus repeatedly gave me a vision of my heart or core inner self. Invariably, I saw a dungeon surrounded by thick walls. Nothing could penetrate them—not even my pleas for Him to walk through these walls. I knew He could do it as He had demonstrated right after His resurrection. Why didn't He do it, even though I invited Him to?
>
> It wasn't until recently that I began to understand the reason why. The adult self was ready, but some parts of me were not. As a child, I had been repeatedly traumatized—as have all of us to some degree—but without having any awareness of Jesus' presence at the time. After all, I didn't come to know Jesus until I was an adult. My childhood selves had to navigate life without knowing Him as my Friend and Savior. They, too, had to invite Him first, before they could receive His help; for He never forces Himself on anyone.
>
> For example, my first memory is of a traumatic experience I had when I was three years old. I can look back as an adult, remember the hurt, and ask the Lord to heal me. My adult self can forgive the perpetrator and perhaps even rationalize his behavior. But this is only of limited effectiveness.
>
> Why? Because there is a part of me—in this case, the three-year-old Eva—that still has unresolved issues. I needed to go back in time and let the three-year-old talk to

Jesus. Although the adult me assured her that Jesus was with her, little Eva wasn't sure at all. Why hadn't He protected her? Had she done something to deserve the abuse that scarred her so badly? What was she to do with the feelings of hurt, shame, and fear that threatened to overwhelm her?

In my imagination, I was the three-year-old, and I heard Jesus assure me that the abuse was not of Him and that I had done nothing wrong. He didn't rationalize it, but offered to take the pain of shame and hurt away if I trusted Him to do it. I gladly invited Him to do so, and the hurt vanished instantly.

Going even further back...

It began to dawn on me that there were other, even earlier parts of me that didn't know Him. As babies and even before birth, we communicate solely nonverbally. Reason can't reach us, but the Spirit can. During a prayer time just with the Lord, He showed me that I believed that my human father had never really wanted me; once I was born, he was only using me for his own purposes. Interestingly, I had received a prophecy many years ago that said, in effect, that I had internalized the lie that I was unwanted and a mistake. Just declaring that this was a lie didn't change anything, though. Only Jesus, through His Holy Spirit, can go into the innermost recesses of the heart and speak truth. Thus, a few days earlier, I woke up with the words: "Persona non grata (unwanted person)." I knew this was a message from the Lord.

I want to emphasize here that I don't know whether it was objectively true that my human father didn't want me at the time. Since he has long since died, I can't ask him. I can surmise the reasons why he may have felt that way. The important thing is the "vibes" that I picked up even as an unborn child signaled rejection; I interpreted them as being unwanted, and it had a profound impact on me. My mother, too, seemed to have used me to fulfill her needs and longing for love and was incapable of giving me love consistently. Therefore, I never really had my basic need for love met. Jesus took me back to the earliest time in the womb and ministered the love and acceptance of the Father, the Son, and the Holy Spirit to me. This time, my deepest heart was ready to receive Him because earlier childhood parts, like the three-year-old, had been healed and introduced to Him. Before, it had just been the adult asking Him for healing, whereas the child had continued to maintain the walls and blocked Him. That's why my prayer didn't work before.

It's only been a very short while since that prayer. At the end of it, He gave me a vision of a small stream of water cascading into a parched, empty reservoir. His love is beginning to be poured out into my heart, but it will take a while for the water level to rise noticeably. Too much, too fast, would overwhelm me. Jesus is proceeding at my pace, especially since I associate love with violence: "Love violently takes what it wants" was imprinted upon me. This, of course, is a lie. Love is gentle, love gives, and it does not insist on its own way but respects my free will. Love goes at my own pace, not His.

My first impressions are that I now have a spiritual connection with the love of the Father. Before, I could only hear Him say, "I love you," but now there is an additional dimension that never existed before. It feels different than I expected. For the first time, I have a sense of what it means to worship Him in spirit. I'm beginning to sense that His love really does cast out fear, and that I don't have to strive to keep my mind on Him to have peace (Is. 26:3) because His peace is in me.

I'm often asked why someone does not feel the love of God, sense His presence, or why they have not been healed, despite years of prayer and the fact that they know God loves them. In many cases, it is because a wounded part of their soul has rejected God without their knowledge. When the wounded alter (or fragment) is identified and healed, the obstruction to God's goodness is removed.

CHAPTER TWENTY-ONE

Jesus Heals and Integrates an Alter

THE NEXT TESTIMONY IS FROM a friend named Jenny who has pursued emotional healing for decades. Her journey has included many tragic events that have robbed her of hope. As she persisted, God helped her break through the feelings of hopelessness. Jenny has many alters and fragments, and she is aware of them. Take note of how she finds opportunities to nurture them back to health.

> I have a childhood history of sexual abuse, and I lived in an emotionless home. During a move of the Spirit in the 1990s, I went through deliverance and experienced inner healing. But as the years went on, I fell in and out of depression and despair, out of church, and drifted. Starting in 2013, I had a cluster of traumas and grief in which my entire childhood family died and my house burnt down. Everything I had saved of my family history was vaporized in this fire. I spent a year living in my parent's house while recovering from chronic fatigue, then six months in a camper in the backyard without water while our house was being finished.

I stopped being able to think, to process, to feel, and my memory deteriorated. I lost all emotions, gifting, music, and love for my animals. It was a reduction of life to slogging through the days and trying to stay awake. I saw a couple of therapists and tried anti-depressants, but nothing helped.

Then Praying Medic recommended a podcast hosted by Greg Harvey, and from there, I found one hosted by Lisa Perna. I decided to pray in tongues every day and walk out back to spend time in the trees. I cut out all news and listened to the spoken word of God. I felt life coming back and asked God for my memory back. The Holy Spirit started dropping old praise songs into my head from when I was first saved. I sang them all day. I had many experiences with God building me up through Lisa's prayer broadcast. I had some deliverance, some healing, and then I hit a wall. I felt like my tongue was tied, and I couldn't get anything out into words or writing. I got these horrible negative thoughts that I was a fraud as a Christian and decided to set up a little prayer closet and step things up.

Every day I went and worshipped and read the word and found that I was reading Psalm 139 and the song of Mary from Luke. I couldn't get away from them. These are both prenatal themes. Praying Medic had mentioned alters, and I knew I had fragments of myself that were not functioning. It was obvious. My heart was as cold as a stone, and I even told my daughter I felt like a sociopath because I could not access any emotions. I wondered if this part of me was holding something for me and staying away.

I prayed a confession to the Lord and said, I will not be traumatized anymore by anything. You are with me, and I don't care what man can do. You love me, and that's what I will need from now on, your love and your comfort, and I will not seek it elsewhere. I will go to you and trust you. There is no trauma in the presence of God.

I asked for prayer on Praying Medic's Telegram channel for my fragmented part, and he asked me: "Does the fragment know Jesus?"

There is a part of me that takes over when I fall apart. It's this strong, emotionless robot, and I needed to introduce her to Jesus. The strong pull of the prenatal scriptures seemed to indicate a very early piece of myself, perhaps a part of me that was without language. So, I set out to nurture this part as if I was lovingly parenting a small, hurting child. I put beautiful sparkly lights in my prayer space and a stuffed animal hugging its child. I repeated Psalm 139 and asked the Holy Spirit to comfort me. To bring that part back in, so she could be with me always and not have to hold on to pain and dread anymore, but meet Jesus and give it to him, per Praying Medic's little emotional healing booklet.

Jesus Heals and Integrates an Alter

I told my hurt alter child: "You are loved, you are by design, nothing missing, nothing broken, nothing lacking. I covered you in your Mother's womb. I was there, with my hand upon you. I wrote your whole life with intention before you were formed. You are intentional. You are just what I want you to be. Give all the hurts to me. I already took them for you on the cross. Stop holding them. I did it for you so you could receive my love." I had seen and heard this before, but it wasn't for me. Here, I was speaking it over me. This is for me. I am coming out of agreement with lies and trusting and believing God's loving word.

That day I began to see new things, and I asked God for "fluent elocution" in the place of despair. I felt His presence and got a scripture dropped into my mind. When I spoke the scripture, it came out of my mouth backward. This happens to me when my brain isn't processing right (when a non-language alter is at the helm, perhaps). The word was "perfect love casts out fear," but it came out as "Perfect fear casts out love." I was moved with compassion. The word is true backward and forward. I said, "Yes, if you hold onto fear, you will not feel love. So, give him the fear, and take the love." I repeated it the right way, over and over, and my left brain started tingling and got very warm and felt wonderful. As long as it tingled, I kept repeating it.

This is what I will believe from now on, and I will not believe lies about my Lord anymore. I walked out of that prayer closet and floated through the day. The presence of God bent me like a reed in the wind. His peace was strong. I had a couple of mini visions. I received prophetic revelation, which I haven't had in years. The next night, I had a rough time sleeping.

At 3 am, a horrible thought hit my mind. God hasn't healed you. You are deluded. You are just deceiving yourself into thinking you will ever get better. You are just as mentally screwed now as you always have been. There is no hope for you. And speaking in tongues is worthless, and you should stop.

I lay there as if paralyzed, with no words, no counter, no idea what to do. I tossed and turned fitfully. When I got up, I felt like I had just had my life-demon take a stab at my newly integrated fragment. So, I played the opposite game and decreed God's promises again, and prayed in tongues for a very long time. I worshipped and thanked Jesus for setting me free and placed all the lies I had heard at his feet, and reaffirmed that I refused to believe lies about him or myself anymore.

Writing this is a miracle for me, and not a small one. I have not written a coherent thing in several years. I continued seeing new blips of visions and walking in love and faith. I am not flopping around in defeat. I am a beloved child who had God's hand on me and God's purposes for my future. I will defeat all of my enemies with the blood of the Lamb and the word of my testimony. The gates of hell will not prevail against me.

There was a part of me that did not believe this; a small hidden part. A voice that said, victory is for others, but not for me. This part met Jesus, and He healed me. Without compassion, there is no healing. I am on a journey to a heart of compassion. I will not be comforted by anything else. I seek a heart of flesh that feels. Nothing else can satisfy me.

Once, I remembered the stories of what I was like as a kid. My parents always talked about how strong-willed and hard-headed I was, how I would fight tooth and nail when I wanted something and not let go until I prevailed. I asked myself and the Lord, what happened to that part of me? When did I stop trying to dream? If it wasn't for my awesome husband, I don't know what would have happened to me. I was so beaten down I could barely get through the day.

Please remember this: I have had years of professional counseling and medications. These things made me even more numb. Shutting out the distractions and lies and being intentional with pursuing God's heart with honesty and repentance is healing me, along with help and love from my hubby and these sweet friends online.

Bless you,
Jenny

After receiving this testimony, I asked Jenny the following question: Can I ask how you sensed and communicated with the wounded part of your soul?

This was her reply:

I used a past experience for this. In my first inner healing, my counselor was getting frustrated with my refusal to forgive myself for my past failures. He told me I would not progress until I forgave myself. When I tried, I had a visceral reaction of my throat choking off when I tried to get the words out. I tried again at home, but the same thing happened. Then I asked the Lord for help, and I saw a broken and beaten child curled up in a fetal position, hopeless and unresponsive. I knew that it was me. This child had no help, no knowledge, and no parenting, and had to find her way through a trauma on her own. She became my whipping post. I was horrified to see that I was the one that had bludgeoned her into this condition, and without having any reason

Jesus Heals and Integrates an Alter

to trust or hope, she would not come to me and tell me what she was carrying. I saw that I needed to ask for her forgiveness and become consistent in extending grace and love to her. She needed unconditional love.

When I saw this, I was able to forgive myself. You wouldn't expect an infant to handle rejection well, would you? When I stopped kicking myself and gave Jesus a chance to love me, she started talking. I could take those emotions to Jesus.

I have whole year gaps in my memory. Many of them. If you think about it, that part of you has been holding the bag alone and could really use a friend. This survival machinery was designed to protect us from dying of shock when we are confronted with evil. It is a shield that keeps the toxins from destroying us. But it comes at great expense to our daily functioning, our memory, our energy, our teeth, our holding our hearts open in trust to receive good things.

I also found that placing visual comforts in my prayer room made the healing process go faster. I have a picture of Jesus, the shepherd holding the lamb. I have a sparkly lantern with a deer in snow. These are things that speak to me. You may have your own comfort/peace items. I could never do this out in my house or at my bed. I had to find a little spot where only worship and prayer took place, away from the traffic. This part of you is not in a place of trust. It is hunkered down. Show her that you will greet her with comfort and not hostility. As you ask Jesus for help, you may just get raw emotions or negative feelings about yourself. Just start bringing them and putting them on the cross and thanking Him because He bore those sorrows of yours for you on the cross.

When failure or defeat is a familiar state of being, you often want to think, "Here we go again, getting clobbered and losing the battle like always." I made a shift in this. I said, Lord, you are good, you are going to help me and heal me, and all feelings that come up in me, I am bringing straight to you. You are here for my good and not harm. Journaling helps, and also having someone who has gone through it to talk to. It is too weird for a lot of people to even think about. In both of my experiences with this, I had to overcome obstacles that prevented me from going where I wanted to go. I couldn't communicate. I couldn't say words of forgiveness. I couldn't access emotions. When all else failed, I asked God to look inside my heart and show me any unclean way, and I yielded every cell of my being to him. And I vowed that I would never ever give up until my whole heart was His. I'm a little nervous putting this out here, but you are important to Jesus and to me.

Jenny

Some people find it easy to forgive others, but difficult to forgive themselves. If we want to live in freedom, we must forgive ourselves for our mistakes and accept God's forgiveness as well.

CHAPTER TWENTY-TWO

Anita's Healing and Deliverance

THE FOLLOWING TESTIMONY WAS SUBMITTED by Anita Deely, who was healed and set free of demons while listening to one of my videos.

I want to thank you for bringing me back to God, who came into my life in a very real physical way. I have been chronically ill since childhood due to a troubled childhood and a DNA issue that caused me to be extremely sensitive to environmental toxins, especially mold, heavy metals, and pesticides. I was bedridden off and on from chronic fatigue and other unexplained illness for 10 years, and at one point, I spent three years straight in bed from mold illness and Lyme disease that caused minor brain atrophy. I was allergic to many foods. I had circulation issues, thyroid problems, adrenal problems, and other autoimmune and health issues that multiple doctors were not able to heal. I was near death several times, and I know God saved me through prayer. I developed enhanced senses to protect me from environmental toxins, and I was able to get by through massive supplements, intense avoidance of places, people, and things, a lot of rest, a supportive husband, and a very restrictive diet and lifestyle that made normal living difficult. When I listened to your video about healing from Covid and other conditions, strange things happened to my body involuntarily. Several times my mouth opened very wide when you asked God to take away evil spirits. Then I felt as if God broke me out of prison and was pulling a long black goo snake out of the deepest pits of my stomach, almost beyond me. In a vision, I saw both the snake and God. I had this overwhelming feeling of being found after being abandoned and sobbed uncontrollably in relief. The next few times I listened to the prayer, my body started to shake uncontrollably and contort off and on almost violently, emanating from my stomach area. I was lifted up slightly to a partial sitting position from lying down and bent in half several times in different directions, and my body trembled off and on. I was not in control of the violent movements of my body. I do not have any health problems related to seizures or involuntary movements. I was delivered, born again, and baptized in the holy spirit during these encounters having involuntary contortions and trembling uncontrollably by the Spirit of God.

God has completely turned my life around, and I have been healed physically and emotionally. A veil was lifted from my eyes, and I am seeing life and the spirit in a new way. After physically lifting me up, shaking me, and delivering me from a few nasties, God continued to speak to me while awake and in dreams to direct my healing.

I studied your teachings and joined a new church with a healing ministry. I am seeing miracles in my life almost every day. As a child, I had spiritual gifts but did not understand what they were. They frightened me, and I turned away from them. Now they are back in a big way. I am seeing in the spirit, speaking and singing in tongues, and reading voraciously everything I can to learn more. I talk to God every day. I have had miraculous healing. Twenty years of thyroid medicine, an ultrasound that said my thyroid was atrophied and could not heal, and scores of doctors who told me I could never stop taking thyroid medicine due to Hashimoto's were upstaged. The Lord healed my thyroid in an instant when he pulled that snake demon out of me. My thyroid is completely restored and healed, and I am no longer on any medication or supplements. God had other plans for me. He healed me from all my illnesses and autoimmune issues. Jesus, God, and the Holy Spirit are moving in my life in a big way, helping me, my husband, and my children and I will be forever grateful to you for leading me there. I was searching for peace for years prior, not understanding all I needed was God in my life.

Before I heard your healing prayers, I did not believe in tongues, the healing ministry, demons, generational curses, or have any understanding of a living God and that terminology. I knew nothing outside of the Catholic religion beyond what God spoke

Anita's Healing and Deliverance

to me about personally, and frankly, many times, I did not know it was him speaking. I just thought God was somewhere in heaven and only helped in special circumstances. God had healed me from sickness and near death before, but I had not read much of the Bible beyond what I knew from going to the Catholic church. I did not pray often except in emergencies. I now realize God was with me every day, and his voice was directing me, and he saved me from severe abuse and problems.

I did not know until after being delivered that I was being tormented by demons my whole life without understanding what was happening. When God delivered me, I did not understand what was happening to me. I did not believe in demons. God showed me in a picture vision prior to delivering me, and it happened that way, but I had not read much of the Bible and had no frame of reference. This was very scary to me. I could not concentrate on much else as I felt like it was crazy what was happening to me. God was changing me physically and emotionally, and he was delivering generational demons out of me. After you said you would pray for me, I felt like there were legions of angels by my bed, and Jesus delivered me from death. A large skull demon and hundreds of mini skull demons were pulled out of me by Jesus. It was physically exhausting, and my body was trembling a lot. I felt like they were attached to the core of my being.

During the healing and trembling, I saw a spiritual water with many floating bright lights that looked like tiny stars. Some took on a dove shape. One became an eye that looked at me and through me and blinked. I felt an overwhelming love and peace and often heard God speaking to me through thought impressions. I continue to see the bright lights now when Angels are nearby.

At night I was often tormented by evil spirits. When I tried to cast them out, they grabbed my tongue, and I could not speak. They grabbed my feet, caused pain, nightmares, and intense fear. I was seeing portals and symbols when I closed my eyes. I had to have the healing ministry physically lay hands on me and anoint me with oil and pray over me the blood of Jesus to make them go away. I listened to your prayers to keep them away. At one point, the Holy Spirit and Jesus put the Fire of God in me and taught me how to do self-deliverance to cast them out for good. The Lord gave me words of knowledge and led me to freedom as I worked with the Holy Spirit. I learned to pray, to worship, and read the Bible . I developed a real relationship with God.

The generational curses I was healed from are helping my family. After I was delivered, I prayed for my son, and he was instantly healed. My husband saw how my body reacted to your prayer. He tried to stop it once by physically lying on top of me, and God lifted both of us up. This manifestation of God on me turned him to God too. It took many prayers to heal me to this point. Sometimes I was too exhausted to participate, and God would come anyway and shake me until I listened to your prayer and then shake me more during the prayer. God led me to study healing and deliverance and to get free from my emotional trauma.

Prior to finding you, I was having dreams of observing demons in the third person. I think God was showing me what was in me. At one point, they started to attack me when they saw I could see them. Your Covid prayer brought the manifest presence of God to me for healing and deliverance, and I am forever grateful to you for bridging the gap and bringing me closer to God. I am now an on-fire born-again believer praying for salvation, healing, and deliverance for others. The Lord has taught me so much. My life has been completely changed by the power of God. I have been saved, healed, delivered, made whole, and he is healing my family. I am blessed and forever grateful to you. Praise the Lord!

CHAPTER TWENTY-THREE

Diana Jamerson's Testimony

I'VE KNOWN DIANA JAMERSON AND her husband John for more than 10 years. They teach others to heal the sick and have a successful ministry of their own. Diana felt she needed help with healing, so she sought assistance from a ministry called Freedom Encounters. I often recommend Freedom Encounters to those who want one-on-one healing or deliverance. In her testimony, Diana describes the process that brought her emotional healing and deliverance.

> A friend had gone through deliverance with this ministry (Freedom Encounters) over a year ago, and I had seen an incredible change in her life. She had been diagnosed with bi-polar 20 years ago. She was on medications all that time and she was in psychotherapy for over 10 years. She told me about the ministry that she went through, and I prayed for a year about going through their program. There was not any one thing that I could put my finger on that was a huge issue for me. Rather, there were several subtle things that were keeping me from getting complete resolution. I had good results from

past issues by renewing my mind to my identity in the Lord and walking in it, but it was still a daily fight. In January of this year, I sensed the Lord drawing me back to look into this ministry, and then one day, after I asked Him if it was something I should do, He said "yes." In March of 2016, I underwent deliverance, and my alters were healed and integrated. It was very different from any ministry I've ever seen or participated in.

How the Ministry Works: You agree to watch a video conference through their website called Victory Over Spiritual Conflict. They send you a manual to read. When you're done, you follow up if you want to undergo prayer for healing and deliverance. Through the video conference, I watched a teaching on alters and cried during the entire thing. It made so much sense and answered so many of the questions I had about my own personality, my fears, and my anger issues. I prayed and heard from the Lord to go through with deliverance.

The prayer model used by Freedom Encounters has three people ministering to you at the same time. One person is a scribe. They write everything down to create a record for the person being ministered to. The second person leads the ministry encounter. The third person is either a trainee or a coach who assists. The session starts with an explanation of how the process will run. The one receiving prayer must agree to the process. Then they ask the person being prayed for to "go back" and be with Jesus, while they bring the "head" demon to task. (The head demon is the one who is in charge of all the other demons that are affecting your life.) The leader asks Holy Spirit to bind the head demon and bring him before the throne of Father God. Next, the person being prayed for simply reports what they hear, which is the head demon speaking.

The leader requires the head demon to confess what the demonic host has done in your life to physically, mentally, spiritually, and emotionally keep you from the gifts and calling of God on your life. They require the head demon to confess what those giftings and callings are that they were assigned to destroy. The leader then requires the head demon to confess that everything it said was true by swearing by The Lord Jesus Christ of Nazareth, who came in the flesh.

After the head demon has confessed everything required of him by the Lord Jesus, the leader either sends him and the rest of the demons to the throne of Father God for righteous judgment or in my case, 85% of his demonic cadre were destroyed by the fire of Holy Spirit for refusing to cooperate with what the Lord Jesus required. In my case, the head demon finally cooperated and was sent to the throne of Father God with only 15% of the original demons. I felt them leave me. It was like a pressure sensation throughout my body, unlike anything I've ever felt before.

Diana Jamerson's Testimony

The ones praying for me forbid the demons to manifest any kind of physical things like vomiting, cussing, etc. At one point, I started to jerk a bit, and the coach immediately called the head demon to stop it and burned 20% of his cadre with the fire of God. It stopped, and I was fine the rest of the prayer session. Also, I was coherent and aware through the whole prayer session. There was no hypnosis, and nothing was done without my expressed permission.

After that, while I was still with Jesus, they spoke to the Holy Spirit and asked Him about some personal issues that I had wanted to know about. They also asked Him about any false cores or alters. I did have some of those, and He integrated them back into my core. The Holy Spirit gave a list of the gifts that I have and the calling that's on my life. They sealed the ministry as being done, and I agreed in prayer for all that Jesus accomplished.

I went home feeling good, but a bit tired. I started to get John (my husband) ready for bed, and I kept having to remember all the steps to his care and what order I have always done them in. (He is quadriplegic) I've done his care all by myself for 16 years. Everything I had always used looked completely foreign to me. I kept asking Jesus to help me, and He did. The same thing happened the next morning, but it didn't freak me out. I actually felt free.

I've lived with obsessive-compulsive disorder and tried to get free of it before, but never succeeded. I tied my own value to how things were done. I always felt anxious if things were not done in "just the right way," which was my way. All of this was suddenly gone! The anxiety about if there were dishes in the sink or a million other daily things I worried about was totally gone. That was the first significant change I saw, other than the subtle feeling of being very "light."

The next sign of freedom that I noticed was the constant running dialogue in my head about how worthless I was and a million other condemning things. All of that was gone too! It is so nice and quiet in my mind now without the constant negative voices coming at me. There are many other things I could share, but there isn't space here to tell you about all of them. I just want to give you some idea of what freedom feels like.

I attended an "aftercare" meeting five days after my initial prayer session, where they ministered more inner healing, dealt with some children alters, and taught me how to test the spirits that speak to me. One of the giftings that the Lord spoke about in my prayer session was that I heard Him well and that I would be hearing Him even more clearly now. I sensed that very thing last night while teaching a healing class online and praying for people. The ministry gave me a lot of direction for staying clean, praying against the attacks that come from the enemy, and some really powerful warfare prayers. They encouraged me to focus my attention on Jesus and the intimacy of my relationship with Him to keep me strong. They stressed that I should not look to the person who did my prayer session. They're available if you have any questions or if something comes up, but they diligently turn you back to Jesus as much as possible because He is the deliverer, not them.

My life has completely changed, and I know that I am on the right path to walk out my gifts and calling. Praise God!

* Please know that I am not trying to "sell" this ministry. I just needed to give honor where honor is due and be honest in regard to how the alters in my life were integrated.

At the time of this writing, it has been seven years since I went through the process, and not only am I still free, but I am continuing to grow in my truest identity. I think that it's important for people to know that because Jesus spoke of "fruit that lasts." Some deliverance ministries have the same people back like a revolving door. This should not be.

It can be beneficial to receive assistance from a full-time ministry like Freedom Encounters. This is especially true if they teach you about the dynamics of emotional healing and deliverance. This information can help you receive healing from Jesus without assistance after you've learned how to connect with Him. That way, when something new comes up, there's no need to rely on others to help you.

CHAPTER TWENTY-FOUR

Angels Help with Deliverance

IT IS THE BELIEVER'S RESPONSIBILITY to educate others about the true nature of the spiritual world. Some will never know about the existence of evil spirits and how they afflict us if we do not tell them. Once we have informed someone about the existence of demons, it's up to them to decide if they want to be set free. We may want them to be delivered from oppression, but ultimately, they must make that choice. Once they decide they want to be set free, we can exercise authority and evict whatever evil spirits are present. Sometimes, demons will leave immediately, but it may be a gradual process. Occasionally, angels may assist, as they did in the following testimony from Robert.

> In October of 1985, I began working for a construction company as a carpenter. I was assigned to work with a carpenter named Jolie. As we worked together, before long, she began to share with me about Jesus, hearing the word of God from one day to the next. A deep hunger began to well up within me as each day passed to the next.

After a week working together, one morning Jolie shared about demons and how they're everywhere and in everything. I was, of course, very skeptical. So then, with sudden quickening of the Holy Spirit, the truth came out, which would alter my whole life in ways I never thought possible.

She then turned to me and said, "Robert, you have demons, and you need them out." And without really thinking it through, it fell right out of my mouth: "If I have any demons, I want them out." Jolie reached out her hand toward me with a simple prayer, "Giving notice to all demons in me to leave."

Of course, at the time, I had no idea what I was getting into. The Lord almighty had something in store for me. Something happened that I will never forget as long as I live. After work that day, as I was coming home, I had a lot of things on my mind about what Jolie shared. It just seemed like every word that proceeded out of her mouth resonated with me. Something inside of me wanted to make some changes in my life, but I didn't know how.

That night, well into the evening, it must have been about 3:00 am. I was awakened with my hands and feet being held down by angels. Not a little bit freaked out, the angels let go of me. Then after a moment of calming down, I began to sense the presence of God in the room, and I was not afraid. I said, "If that's you, Lord, take the fear away". Then suddenly, the angels began to hold me down again at my hands and feet. With no fear in me, my whole body began to rise off the bed except for my hands and feet.

With my body arched up and with my mouth stretched wide open, several demons violently roared out of me. I then simply fell back to sleep. Waking up that morning, and as I sat up, the whole room was filled with the fragrance of roses. I quickly stepped out of bed and suddenly realized my feet did not feel like they were touching the ground. As I looked down, they were on the ground, but I felt like I was two feet off the ground all day long. I have come to know the true meaning of being set free. Thank you Jesus!

CHAPTER TWENTY-FIVE

The Spectrum of Mind Control

As a paramedic, I've been trained to carry out certain actions when faced with a particular situation. When I encounter someone in cardiac arrest, I intuitively follow the steps outlined in the American Heart Association cardiac arrest protocol. When caring for someone with a skull fracture, I automatically follow a protocol for treating head injuries. Paramedics are trained to follow protocols for nearly every type of medical emergency. Protocols provide a standardized set of responses to a given situation. They take the guesswork out of decision-making in situations where stress can cloud judgment. They are an example of how we can be programmed to think and act a certain way.

Programming can be thought of as learned behavior. We learn to respond to a variety of situations due to the programming we've received during our lifetime. Programmed learning is a necessary part of society. The CEO of a company would be foolish to let his employees behave however they wanted. A productive work environment is created by defining desirable behaviors and ones that are unacceptable. Employees who perform well are rewarded. Those who do not are punished. As noted by psychologist B.F. Skinner, reward and punishment are at the heart of behavioral conditioning.

Behavioral conditioning is used when one wants to direct or alter the behavior of another. Parents use it to encourage good behavior in their children. Spouses may use it to obtain favor from their mates. But when it is used to control others for a malevolent purpose, it may be a subtle form of mind control. I'd like to provide a few examples of how behavioral conditioning can be misused.

I frequently receive emails from individuals whose spouses allow themselves to be manipulated by controlling parents. Typically, the one being controlled is rewarded by a parent with praise or affection for their obedience, and affection is withdrawn when a demand goes unheeded. The downside of non-compliance in a control-based relationship is the risk of a damaged or severed relationship. The upside of non-compliance is the freedom to do as one pleases. Because they fear rejection, the one being controlled submits. When we are young, it's normal to follow the advice of a parent, but a 50-year-old man who follows his mother's wishes without question may be the victim of a subtle form of mind control. (Strategies for freeing yourself from controlling personal relationships can be found in the *Boundaries* books by Henry Cloud and John Townsend.)

Many people have suffered what they perceive to be mental abuse at the hands of church leaders. Most often, it amounts to a heavy-handed use of control and manipulation through reward and punishment. Most church leaders who engage in such practices do not intend to inflict emotional trauma on others. But there is a broadly accepted way of dealing with church members who are perceived to be troublemakers. Good behavior is rewarded, while bad behavior is punished. Leaders don't see themselves as controlling abusers. And the abused don't see themselves as troublesome. Yet, the dynamic is observable and widespread. Behavior that aims to control groups of people is not limited to religion. It is alive and well in other areas of society—including politics and entertainment.

The Spectrum of Mind Control

Years ago, I followed someone on social media who hosted weekly live broadcasts. This person had unique insights into politics, and I was interested in learning more. Those who followed this leader became friends with each other online. They discussed subjects of interest in chat groups. Later, these followers learned that a handful of people had been designated to steer the conversations in the chat groups. These individuals pushed back on the opinions of followers that were contrary to the leader's opinion. They took screenshots of chat conversations and forwarded those screenshots to the leader. The leader would then humiliate people on live broadcasts over the wrong ideas they shared. Right thinking and loyalty to the leader were rewarded publicly. Wrong thinking and disloyalty were punished. Since then, I've encountered the same dynamic in other groups that follow political personalities.

This type of emotional abuse lies at one end of the mind control spectrum, where religious and political cults use reward and punishment as a broad policy on all members. Indoctrination and behavior modification are universally applied, but physical abuse is absent. Moving further down the spectrum, we find groups that use physical abuse to modify the behavior of members. Next are groups that program members to perform sex acts on demand. At the far end of the spectrum are cults that exert control over every aspect of the lives of their members.

Minor forms of emotional trauma caused by mind control can be healed using the techniques outlined in previous chapters. But the mental programming used by sex cults and secret societies requires a different approach. Such programming often includes techniques that will cause the individual to commit suicide when attempts are made to undo their programming. Because the risk of suicide is high in these individuals, extreme caution must be exercised. In the following chapters, we'll hear from a woman who performed such programming. She'll describe the techniques she used to program cult members, and we'll look at strategies for helping them obtain healing.

CHAPTER TWENTY-SIX

Svali – A Former Illuminati Trainer

IN KEEPING WITH THE THEME of sharing personal testimonies, the next few chapters will include testimonies from a woman who was born into the Illuminati cult and rose to a position where she trained others to inflict trauma-based mind control.

To be perfectly honest, I've never had much interest in the Illuminati or secret societies in general. As a researcher, I've read articles on the subject. But I've found it difficult to take people's claims about the Illuminati seriously. One of my concerns is the many claims that have been made which can't be verified. It's been difficult (for me) to find an account that explains the Illuminati's history, goals, strategies, and tactics in a concise, factual, and objective way.

Despite my indifference to the Illuminati, while researching trauma-based mind control, I found a series of articles and books written by a woman

123

who assumed the pen name Svali. She says she was born into the Illuminati cult and escaped in 1995 at the age of 38. After leaving the cult, she wrote extensively on several websites about the Illuminati, with focus on the way the group programs its members.

I read her material with a healthy dose of skepticism at first. But after evaluating a larger volume of her books and articles, I've found her testimony consistent and free from contradictions. In my opinion, Svali writes objectively and factually. She avoids sensationalism and, in some cases, downplays issues that others have sensationalized. I appreciate her organized and methodical treatment of the topics she discusses in her writing.

I find Svali to be a credible witness. I contacted her and received permission to paraphrase and use direct quotes from her material. In the chapters that follow, I'll provide excerpts from her articles and interviews, and I'll paraphrase information found in her books. My goal is not to explain every aspect of the Illuminati. (If you'd like to learn more about this subject, I recommend reading her books and articles, but be advised that her material contains graphic descriptions.) The focus of this book is emotional healing and deliverance. So, her testimonies will be limited to those that describe the techniques used to program human subjects and tips on setting them free.

Svali's books:
Svali Speaks - Breaking Free of Cult Programming
It's Not Impossible - Healing from Mind Control and Ritual Abuse
The Svali Chronicles - Breaking Free From Mind Control

Svali's website: https://svalispeaksagain.wordpress.com/

Important Warning: Sensitive Content

Up to this point, the information in this book has been suitable for all readers. What follows is not suitable for everyone. The next chapter provides terms and definitions that will help readers understand the information in the chapters that follow. Chapters 28-31 contain passages that describe torture and abuse perpetrated during childhood and beyond. I've tried as much as possible to limit the inclusion of gruesome details. But some graphic descriptions are necessary to convey the essence of the matter—and to understand how to help those who have suffered this trauma.

If you are not in a position to help ritual abuse survivors with healing, you may not need this information. If you are a survivor of abuse, you may be triggered while reading and have thoughts of self-harm. Please consider avoiding chapters with a Sensitive Content warning at the beginning, or read them with someone who can provide immediate help. If you have a sensitive nature, you may find the material repugnant or frightening. If the information about ritual abuse is likely to cause you discomfort, I invite you to skip to chapter 34.

CHAPTER TWENTY-SEVEN

Trauma-Based Mind Control: Terminology

WARNING: SENSITIVE CONTENT — *This chapter contains definitions related to dissociation caused by trauma.*

THOSE WHO DISCUSS MIND CONTROL use terms that have a meaning other than what they mean to the general public. It's easy to become confused when reading about this subject. To understand the concepts presented in the following chapters (and Svali's articles and books), you'll need to become familiar with the contextual meaning of a number of terms. This chapter provides a list of terms and definitions commonly used in treating trauma-based mind control.

Subject - An individual who receives mind control programming.

Survivor - Someone who has survived ritual abuse or trauma-based mind control.

Alter - When emotional trauma occurs, the soul can be fragmented into different parts. An alter is a part of the soul that develops its own personality, thoughts, feelings, memories, preferences, abilities, ideas of self, and illnesses. Alters may assume control of the individual's responses to the outside world, or they may perform tasks internally.

Fragment - A part of the soul created by emotional trauma. Fragments often hold a single memory, handle a single emotion, or perform a specific task. They can vary in complexity but are generally less developed than alters.

Core or Original - The original persona that was born with the physical body. The core is usually the main personality.

Core Split - An alter that is created by traumatizing the core.

System - A collection of alters within the body. Some individuals have multiple systems of alters. Where multiple systems exist, each is created for a unique purpose.

Sub-System - A small group of alters within a larger group (system) of alters.

Front System - A group of alters that are regularly in control of the physical body.

Back System - A group of alters that do not assume control of the body. They manage the internal affairs of the individual and are usually involved in cult activity.

Front - A term that describes interactions with the physical world.

Back - A term that describes interactions inside the soul.

Fronting, Hosting, or Presenting - Terms that describe when an alter controls the body and interacts with the physical world. Also referred to as being "out" or being "up."

Host - The alter that controls the body most often.

Presenting Part - The alter that controls the body at a particular time.

Switch - The change where one alter relinquishes control of the body to another alter or the core.

Dissociation - An experience where one feels temporarily disconnected from oneself and their surroundings. It occurs on a spectrum from mild to severe. An example of mild dissociation is daydreaming. An example of severe dissociation is when an alter assumes control of the body for several days, leaving the core persona with amnesia of what happened during that time.

Shell or Mask Alter - An alter that allows other alters to speak through them, thus, concealing the identities of these alters from the outside world.

Introject - An alter that has an identity resembling that of someone outside the system, such as a programmer.

Fictive - An alter that assumes the identity of a fictional character.

Co-hosting or Co-fronting - When two or more alters control the body at the same time.

Co-aware or Co-conscious - When alters in a system are aware of each other, what is happening in the system, and what other alters are doing.

Integration - Where two or more alters merge into one or where an alter merges with the core.

Inside or Inner World - The internal world where alters exist.

Trigger - A stimulus that sets in motion a programmed routine or reminds a person of some aspect of their traumatic past. A trigger may cause a panic attack, flashback, dissociation, or a switch. When something is written that could cause a trigger, a warning should be provided.

Computer - An alter (or system) programmed to run various routines as directed by a trainer.

EMOTIONAL HEALING AND DELIVERANCE MADE SIMPLE

Program - A method of causing a person to think and act a certain way. Mind control programs are induced through techniques such as punishment (torture), reward, indoctrination, and hypnosis.

Code - Programming that uses numbers, colors, phrases, gestures, patterns, playing cards, dice, clocks, or other stimuli to signal to an individual to carry out a specific action.

Function Code - Programming that instructs a mind control subject how and when to perform assigned jobs and tasks.

Command Code - A signal associated with a program that directs a subject to perform or halt a specific task.

Suicide Code - Programming that causes an alter or fragment to assume control of the body and attempt suicide when specific criteria are met.

Access Code - Programming that restricts unauthorized access to the subject's internal programming. Trainers create coded messages that allow them to modify a subject's programming while preventing others from attempting to undo it.

Access - When a member attempts to leave a cult, various programmed methods are used to coerce them to re-establish contact (access) with the cult.

Family - A word used by members to describe the Illuminati cult.

Setup - A situation that a trainer contrives to teach a cult member a lesson, which the member believes to be real.

CHAPTER TWENTY-EIGHT

Methods of Illuminati Programming

> **WARNING: SENSITIVE CONTENT** — *This chapter contains graphic descriptions of ritual abuse. If you are sensitive or you are a survivor of abuse, you may be triggered and have thoughts of self-harm. Please consider avoiding chapters with this warning, or read them with someone who can provide immediate help.*

ACCORDING TO SVALI, THE GOAL of the Illuminati is to control the world. She says that many of the largest banks and financial institutions in the world are controlled by Illuminists. At a future time, they intend to bring about a global financial collapse. During the ensuing chaos, they hope to set up a system of government that spans the globe with their people at the top. Members of the cult are programmed to learn skills that will help them wield control during this time. Svali says that the cult already controls many of the levers of power today. Their control is real, though at present, remains unrecognized by most people.

EMOTIONAL HEALING AND DELIVERANCE *MADE SIMPLE*

At a future time, they intend to make their control publicly known. Although this plan would be deemed evil by most people, members of the cult believe they are called to save mankind from disaster by "bringing order out of chaos"—a mantra that is often recited by them.

Before we examine the techniques of mind control programming, I want to discuss motives. Hollywood films often portray villains as heartless individuals who want nothing more than to inflict pain on others. It would be easy to cast mind control programmers in that same light, but such a characterization may not be accurate. According to her testimony, Svali carried on the work of the famous Nazi scientist Joseph Mengele. Her job was to develop methods of mind control programming, evaluate them clinically, and make modifications to enhance their effectiveness. Methods that produced poor results were abandoned. Those that showed promise were improved upon. Her goal was not to develop the most cruel or the most painful methods possible. It was to develop methods that produced the most consistent, long-lasting results in the most efficient manner possible—irrespective of whether they caused pain. And while it is true that the methods she implemented *did* cause pain and suffering, that was not her goal. Her goal was to bring her subjects under her control; she was raised by the family/cult to do this, and she was also subjected to this abuse as a child.

Svali highlights the upside-down reality of life inside the cult. She says that, on the whole, members do not see their actions as evil. On the contrary, they see themselves as a positive force in society. They're programmed from infancy to believe that the torment they endure and that which they inflict on others has the effect of making them stronger. They're programmed to think that they are the solution to society's ills. They sincerely believe that what they are doing is morally right. What does one do when they are programmed to believe that wrong is right and right is wrong? Svali points out that if members had an inkling that what they were doing was wrong, they would not be able to continue doing it. And in fact, when a cult member does suspect that what they are doing *is* wrong, they wrestle with what they've been taught about the cult. If their concerns persist, they typically begin making plans to leave. When Svali became a Christian, the Holy Spirit convinced her that what she was doing was wrong. That set into motion her plans to get out of the cult. To be clear: I'm not making excuses for the behavior of

Methods of Illuminati Programming

these individuals. Mind control programming is a reprehensible practice. But, for the purpose of learning, it may help to keep the motives of its practitioners in the proper perspective.

Svali describes the mind control methods used by a particular cult, but similar techniques are used by other secret societies. Unlike many cults, the Illuminati do not recruit members from society. When a member is born, they are dedicated to the cult by their parents, who were dedicated by their parents, who were likewise dedicated by their parents. All the members of a family—grandparents, aunts, uncles, parents, cousins, brothers, sisters, and children are cult members. For this reason, the Illuminati is considered a trans-generational cult. Once you're a member, their desire is to make sure you remain a member for life. Svali says that nearly all marriages within the cult are arranged. Members are not allowed to marry outside the "family."

Members lead different lives during the daytime and nighttime. During the day, their activities may appear normal to the outsider. Ceremonies, rituals, meetings, and instruction generally occur at night in secluded locations. Many members have one set of alters that handle daytime activities and a different set of alters that engage in nocturnal cult activities. The cult has many activities in which members are expected to participate. Unique alters are created that participate in each activity.

The mental programming of the Illuminati takes a variety of forms. The following chapters will explain some of the most common forms of programming and why they are used.

An *unintentional* kind of programming occurs in the daily life of children born into the cult. Children are raised in an environment that features daytime abandonment from dysfunctional, dissociated parents, who act one way at home during the day, a different way at cult gatherings, and yet another way outside the home during work hours or social activities. The infant may be deprived of attention or abused during the daytime and given special attention during nighttime cult activities. The child learns that the nighttime cult activities are the important ones. Abandonment, confusion, and abuse lead to the formation of fragments, including those that crave the attention they receive at night. The child is unintentionally conditioned to believe that adults are unpredictable, unreliable, and untrustworthy. The frequent switching of alters in parents sets up a pattern for a traumatized child to follow.

Intentional programming often begins before birth. The prenatal development of alters is well known; a fetus is capable of fragmenting in the womb when subjected to trauma. Techniques used to induce trauma include placing headphones on the mother's abdomen and playing loud music or yelling at the fetus inside the womb. The mother's abdomen may be hit or mild shock may be applied. Electric shock may be used to cause premature labor, which may ensure that the infant is born on a ceremonial holiday. Or, labor-inducing drugs may be given if a certain birth date is desired.

Once the infant is born, aptitude testing begins. Trainers are taught to look for specific abilities. They will place the child on a velvet cloth on a table and observe the infant's reflexes to different stimuli. Strength is measured, and reactions to heat, cold, and pain are evaluated. Trainers look for dissociative ability, quick reflexes, and reaction times. The tests also encourage early dissociation.

The infant will be abused to create fragments—including sexually. Methods of abuse can include probes; electric shock at a low level to the fingers, toes, and genitals, and cutting the genitalia. The intent is to condition the child to create fragments in response to pain. Infants will be intentionally abandoned or uncared for during the daytime and then picked up, soothed, and given attention while preparing for a ritual or group gathering at night. This is done to condition them to associate night gatherings with love, attention, and security, creating a stronger loyalty bond to the cult.

As the child grows older, they will be subjected to alternating periods where they'll first be soothed and then given electric shocks to their fingers. They may be dropped from heights to a mat and mocked when they cry. They will be placed in cages and deprived of food, water, and basic needs, all in an attempt to induce dissociation. All cult members receive programming through what Svali calls "The 12 Steps of Discipline"—a progressive path of conditioning that culminates in a "coming of age" ceremony. The steps may vary from one region to another depending on the needs and preferences of trainers and parents.

Methods of Illuminati Programming

Step One: To Not Need

The toddler will be placed in a room without sensory stimuli, usually a training room with gray, white, or beige walls. The adult will leave, and the child will be alone for several hours—or when the child grows older, an entire day. If the child begs the adult to stay or if they scream, they are beaten and told that the time of isolation will increase until they learn to stop being weak. The goal is to teach them to ignore their own needs, which is said to strengthen them. In the process, trauma is induced, and fragments are created. When the trainer returns to the room, the child is often found rocking or hugging themselves in a corner, nearly catatonic. The trainer will then "rescue" the child, feed them, give them something to drink, and bond with a child who now sees them as their savior. The trainer will say that the "family" (the Illuminati) told them to rescue the child because the family loves them. The trainer will then instill in them the key teachings of the cult.

Step Two: To Not Want

The second step is done concurrently with the first step. The child is left alone in a room, without food or water for long periods of time. An adult will enter with a large pitcher of water or food. If the child asks for either, the adult, who is eating or drinking in front of them, will punish them for being weak and needy. This dynamic is repeated until the child learns not to ask for food or water unless it is offered. The rationale is that it creates a child who is mentally strong. The process induces dissociation and teaches the child to look for cues from other cult members about their bodily needs. They're conditioned to suppress their needs until someone else tells them it's okay to fulfill them.

Step Three: To Not Wish

A child will be placed in a room with favorite toys, and an adult will join them. They'll engage in fantasy play about the child's secret wishes, dreams, or wants. This will be done several times as the child's trust is earned and information is gleaned about their secret desires. Later, the child will be severely punished over what was shared with the adult, including destroying their favorite toys, undoing or destroying secret safe places the child may have created inside themselves, or destroying protector alters that are not loyal to the cult. This step is repeated, with variations, many times. The child's siblings, parents, or friends will be used to obtain inside fantasies revealed to them during the daytime or in unguarded moments. The reason the cult gives for this step is to create a child who doesn't fantasize—one who is more outwardly and less inwardly directed. The child must look to adult cult members for permission in all aspects of his life while suppressing internal desires. The child is conditioned to believe that there is no true safety and that the cult will find out everything they think. Exercises like this are used to create alters who will report to trainers any secret wishes the child has against the cult.

Step Four: The Survival of the Fittest

The first three steps may create rage in the child. That rage is directed in the fourth step. All cult members are trained to inflict pain on others. The fourth step creates perpetrator alters. A child will be brought into a room with a trainer and another child of the same age or slightly younger. The subject child will be severely beaten by the trainer, then told to hit the other child, or they will be beaten again. If the child refuses, they are punished, and the other child is punished as well. Then the subject child is told to beat the other child. If they refuse, cry, or hit the trainer instead, they are severely beaten, and then told to direct their anger at the other child and beat them. This is repeated until the child complies. This conditioning begins around age two and is used to create aggressive perpetrator alters. As they age, the punishment becomes more brutal, and they will practice on children younger than themselves. Aggressive behavior is rewarded. The child learns that this is the acceptable outlet for the aggressive impulses and rage created by the brutality they experience.

Step Five: The Code of Silence

After a ritual or group gathering, the child will be asked about what they saw or heard during the meeting. When they comply, they are severely beaten or tortured. A new alter is created, who is told to guard the memories of what was seen or heard and never disclose them to anyone unless they want to die. The new alter agrees to secrecy. The child and the new alter are put through a ceremony of swearing to never ever tell. Alters are created whose job it is to kill the body if other alters remember and disclose certain events. The child endures torture to ensure that they will never tell a secret. The torture may include being buried alive, near drowning, watching "traitor's deaths" involving slow, painful torture, such as being burned, or skinned alive, being buried with a partially rotted corpse, and being told that they will become a corpse if they ever tell.

The cult is involved in criminal activities and must ensure the silence of its members. This is why the cult has survived so long under a shroud of secrecy and why more members do not leave or discuss their experiences. Members are told that they will be hunted down and killed if they ever tell. The assassin training they experience later lets them know that it is not an idle threat. The child will be exposed to many role-playing situations that reinforce this programming.

Step Six: Betrayal Programming

One goal of the Illuminati is to instill undying loyalty to the cult and its members. A member who is loyal to another human may one day turn against the cult. Thus, the cult must program its members to value the betrayal of others for the good of the "family." A child learns betrayal through what Svali calls "setups"—contrived situations that the subject believes are real.

A child will be placed in situations where an adult who seems kind will rescue them and gain their trust. After the adult intervenes several times, the child will view them as a kind of savior. After a period of bonding, one day, the child will turn to the adult for help, but the adult will back away, mock the child and abuse them. This creates a programmed belief that adults cannot be trusted.

Another setup involves what is referred to as "twinning." Ideally, this is done with biological twins, but that is not always possible. A child will be allowed to play with and become close to another child in the cult. At some point, the child will be told that the other child is their twin and that they were separated at birth. It is explained that this is a secret, and they are instructed not to tell anyone, or they will be punished. The child is usually overjoyed. The children will be taught together and do military training together.

But at some point, they will be forced to hurt each other. If one "twin" is considered to be expendable, a situation will be created where one twin will die while the other watches. One twin may be forced to gather secrets from the other and disclose them to a trainer. In this situation, one twin will be forced to kill the other one. In other cases, one twin will be forced to beat the other. If they refuse, the trainer will brutalize one twin, and the refusing twin will be told that their "twin" was hurt because of their refusal. This programming conditions them to trust no one.

Step Seven: Not Caring

The seventh step reinforces perpetrator alters. The child will be forced to hurt others and remain indifferent.

Step Eight: Time Travel

The child will be taught principles of spiritual traveling through contrived situations, role-playing, and guided exercises. The goal is to attain enlightenment, which is done by traveling in time to witness ancient rituals and teachings. Svali says illuminists can travel backward in time without restriction, and forward in time with limitations. She notes that this kind of spiritual travel causes the body to age rapidly. Cult members who travel in the spirit tend to have white hair at a young age. Thus, they limit this practice. (In my book, *Traveling in the Spirit Made Simple*, I share many testimonies from Christians who travel in the spirit. **NOTE:** Premature aging associated with spiritual travel is unknown to those of us in the Christian community, probably because our spiritual travel does not include the practice of astral projection, which is frequently practiced by Illuminati cult members.)

Methods of Illuminati Programming

Steps Nine, Ten, and Eleven: Further Preparation

These steps involve programming that varies according to the child's future role in the cult. They include sexual trauma, learning to dissociate, and increasing cognition. Decreasing emotional responses to trauma is emphasized in these steps as well.

Step Twelve: "Coming of Age"

A ceremony is held at age twelve or thirteen, where the child is formally inducted into the cult, and their adult role is recognized. They must prove their ability by demonstrating proficiency in their role to the satisfaction of their trainer and cult leaders. They'll participate in a special induction ceremony. Other children their age will participate in the ceremony as well. Prizes are awarded to acknowledge the successful completion of training. The child will continue to be abused, even into adulthood, but the major trauma and creation of systems of alters will be complete.

❖ Suggestions for Helping Survivors ❖

- *Svali's suggestions* for helping survivors will be found at the end of certain upcoming chapters, where appropriate.

- *My approach* to healing can be found in chapter 33.

Svali offers the following advice for assisting survivors who have been programmed using the 12 steps outlined above (or similar programming):

"Grieving the abuse, and acknowledging the feelings associated with undergoing the trauma will be important. It will be necessary to deal with perpetrator guilt since, by this time, the child will be a perpetrator and will have identified with the adult role models around them. This can be difficult to do since perpetration will horrify the survivor when they remember this. Supporting the survivor, remaining non-judgmental, and encouraging acceptance of these parts is important. Pointing out that, at the time, they saw

no other options available will help. Realizing that perpetrator alters saved the child's life and that they had no other way to act, especially originally, the first time, will need to be pointed out. The survivor may feel hostile toward or reviled by perpetrator alters, but they are the expression of the abuse and limited choices they were allowed. Grieving being a perpetrator will take time and caring support by others."

Svali continues:

"Allow these parts to slowly acknowledge the agony that they experienced during their deprivation: heat (being held over a fire or stove); cold (such as being placed in freezers, or ice, for example), lack of food, etc. Encourage the sharing of the cognitive portion of the memories first while allowing amnesic alters to grieve over 'hearing about' these things. Allow them time to absorb hearing about these traumas, as they occurred over several years during early childhood and will take time to assimilate.

Healing can't be rushed. Allow feeling alters later to step forward and share their feelings while more cognitive or helper parts are inside holding their hands, grounding them to the here and now throughout the process of remembering. Be prepared for floods of emotion at times, as well as body memories, as the abuse is recalled. A group of alters can be designated as a 'grounding team' to help ground these parts as they step forward and share their memories."

Svali adds this reminder:

"External safety is paramount to undoing inside programming. You have to be able to promise these parts external safety and deliver on this promise, or they will understandably balk at working inside on undoing programming. Why should they try and change, only to go back and be punished again? No system will undo its own protective dissociation if the abuse is ongoing, or it will continue to destabilize and re-dissociate over and over. This is because dismantling the dissociation would mean dismantling its own survival and protection. Stopping contact with perpetrators and having a safe therapist are the very first steps to take before attempting to

undo internal programming. A system can still work on stopping cult contact and begin healing while being accessed, but it will slow therapy down tremendously as the internal energy will be diverted to staying safe rather than undoing trauma. A person can heal, and most survivors are still in cult contact when they enter therapy. But the progress will go much more quickly once cult contact is broken."

CHAPTER TWENTY-NINE

Programming Themes and Internal Structures

WARNING: SENSITIVE CONTENT — *This chapter contains graphic descriptions of ritual abuse. If you are sensitive or you are a survivor of abuse, you may be triggered and have thoughts of self-harm. Please consider avoiding chapters with this warning, or read them with someone who can provide immediate help.*

AT THIS POINT, IT WILL help to explain how a programmer communicates with alters and gets them to come up on command. Svali says that trainers read a subject's body language, and they exercise spiritual discernment when it comes to bringing a part forward:

"After trauma that creates structured dissociation, the part is a 'blank slate' and very amenable to outside suggestion (also, the child is very, very young normally, even an infant, when this process is started). Immediately, the part is given a name and codes

> *that bring it out. The part is also bonded with the trainer after the trauma (the part is comforted, held, etc.). In occultic groups, a ritual is also done to attach a spirit (demon) to this new part. The spirit then helps to 'bring' the part forward in the future.*
>
> *After this process, there is no need to re-traumatize to bring the part out; the trainer may do a short ritual to the spirit, then ask it to bring forward the part in the person; over time, the codes are also used to bring the part out (such as a color, a number, a specific pattern, etc., along with a series of tones for some groups). In time, the part may be brought out on request with help of an alter that serves as a system controller."*

Svali says that rituals are performed before and after sessions of abuse that serve to summon demons and seal the programming in the soul of the victim. These rituals may include animal or other types of sacrifice. This may be why "ritual abuse" is the most common term used to describe this activity, though personally, I find the term "trauma-based mind control" to be more descriptive of the process.

One can condition an alter to do anything humanly possible. Each unique task given to an alter requires special training. Thus, programmers create separate alters to accomplish different tasks.

Because some jobs require a team of diversely skilled individuals, programmers will create groups of alters that collectively carry out certain assignments. Each group of alters can be thought of as a separate system or subsystem within the individual. Many survivors of ritual abuse have several distinct systems of alters within them.

Alters that are split or created from another alter are relatively weak and unstable. An alter created from the individual's original core is stronger and more stable. When a new system of alters is created, it is preferable to use an alter split from the core persona as the primary alter from which other alters are created for that system. The "core split" alter serves as a kind of template for a system of new alters. Most systems will have alters that serve as controllers. A controller is an alter that directs the activity of a system. They decide which alters can assume control of the body and when.

Programming Themes and Internal Structures

Those who are subjected to ritual abuse may have hundreds or thousands of fragments and alters. If a trainer is to be effective, they must have a good grasp of the systems of alters that exist inside a subject. Trainers do not always work with the same subjects. Thus, maps are created that describe the systems of each cult member. Any trainer can reference a map (also known as a grid) to locate alters within a system. (It is a good idea to create your own map of a person's system if you plan to help deprogram or heal them. Sometimes, a controller alter will be able to assist you in creating it).

Systems of alters are assigned labels. Labels allow trainers to categorize and quickly call up alters within a system. The most common labels are colors, but jewels and metals are also used. Children recognize colors before they can read, so color programming can occur at an early age.

Color Programming

In color programming, a child will be taken into a room with white or neutral-colored walls. The bulbs in the light fixtures will be changed so they bathe the room in the desired color. If blue is the color being programmed, the trainer will call up an alter, usually a controller or core split. They will tell the child that they will learn how to become blue, and what blue means. The trainer will dress in blue clothing and may wear a blue mask. Blue objects will be placed in the room to reinforce the programming. The alter will be called up, and the child will be drugged, hypnotized, and traumatized. As they awaken from the trauma, they are told that blue is good, and that they *are* blue. Blue is important. Blue will protect you from harm. Blue people don't get hurt. The trainer will ask the child if they want to become blue. If they say "yes," the programming will continue. If the child says "no," they will be re-traumatized until they say "yes." The child may be naked and told they cannot wear clothing until they earn the right to wear a blue robe. The safety of being blue and the danger of not being blue is repeated. The alter will eventually want to be blue. When they comply, they may be given blue candy or blue sunglasses and allowed to wear a blue robe.

Once the main alter for a system accepts their color, they will be taught over multiple training sessions what the color means. Part of the pro-

EMOTIONAL HEALING AND DELIVERANCE MADE SIMPLE

gramming involves role playing. Trainers will have their victims act out scenes that reinforce programming. In color programming, cult children who have alters programmed to think they are blue, will act out the role of a "blue" as they are instructed to by a trainer. The child will be drugged, hypnotized, and traumatized while the meaning of blue is programmed into them. Trainers in different regions assign different meanings to colors. When a trainer needs to access a system, they may call them up by color or wear certain colored clothing. The clothing becomes an unconscious trigger for alters of that color to come forward.

Jewel and Metal Programming

Illuminati children may go through either metals or jewels programming (or both). Like all cult programming, it is based on reward and punishment.

A child will be shown a piece of jewelry, such as a ring, or an example of the jewel stone (or metal) that is being programmed. They will be asked: "Isn't this Amethyst beautiful?" The child will be eager to look at and touch it. This will be encouraged. The trainer will ask, "Wouldn't you like to be beautiful, like this jewel?" The child will be eager to comply. The trainer will extol the gem's beauty and tell the child how special and valued gems are. The child will then be told that to become a jewel, they must earn the right. This involves:

1. Passing through the steps of discipline. (See the previous chapter.)
2. Passing special tests.
3. Being rewarded for exceptional achievement.

Over time, and with the help of drugs, hypnosis, shock, and other trauma, the child will complete their training and earn jewels or metals as rewards. The jewels and metals become alters in the same way that color alters are programmed.

Amethyst is usually the first one earned and is linked to keeping secrets. Ruby is reserved for when the child is traumatized sexually and creates sexual alters to please adults. Emerald programming is for young teenagers and is linked to family loyalty, witchcraft, and spiritual achievement. Diamond is the highest gemstone and may not be earned until adulthood. It will be the controlling alter in a gemstone system. A diamond alter will have completed all twelve steps of discipline and other loyalty tests. Metals programming is done similarly to jewels, with bronze being the lowest and platinum being the highest.

Film Programming

Children's movies and books are frequently used in cult programming. Among those most often used are *Fantasia, Alice in Wonderland, Sleeping Beauty, Cinderella,* and *The Wizard of Oz*. A trainer will play a movie for the child who is to be programmed. They are warned that they will be asked about details of the movie, which cues them to use their photographic recall to store as many details as possible. Afterward, they will be chemically sedated and asked what they remember. They will be shocked if they fail to recall important details and are forced to watch the scenes repetitively until they memorize them. When the child has total recall, the trainer will tell them they are one of the characters. The subject may be heavily traumatized first to create a blank slate alter that will assume the character's identity. (An alter that takes the identity of a fictional character is called a "fictive.") The first thing the blank slate alter sees is a scene from the movie featuring the character. This is the alter's first memory. The trainer will then link the scene and its characters to Illuminati ideology. They will teach the child a supposedly hidden meaning of the movie and praise them for being one of the few "enlightened ones" who understand what it truly means.

Internal Structures

Because Illuminati programmers must be able to access alters and fragments when needed, organizational structures are created in the soul that provide locations where they can congregate. Previously, I mentioned that Steve Harmon was told by Jesus to speak into existence a book about God. Our words have creative power. In a similar way, Illuminati trainers create structures inside their subjects that provide locations where alters and fragments can be assigned and called up when needed. If an alter is assigned to a specific temple, for example,

EMOTIONAL HEALING AND DELIVERANCE MADE SIMPLE

a trainer can locate them more easily. These structures also serve to reinforce programming themes.

Temples are often consecrated to principal Illuminati deities. Spiritual alters will congregate there. These may represent actual temples that the person has visited. The temple of Moloch, for example, will be created out of black stone and have a fire burning inside it. Another temple features the all-seeing eye of Horus, one of the most common structures in an Illuminati system. Horus is a deity revered by Illuminists. The all-seeing eye in a system reinforces the idea that the cult can always see what the individual is doing. It also represents being dedicated to Horus in a ceremony. The eye is suggestive that demons continually watch the person's activities.

The Illuminati revere ancient Egyptian symbology. Pyramids will be placed internally as triangles, and pyramids represent strength and stability. Pyramids, triangles, and the number three represent calling up the demonic in Illuminist philosophy.

A system of alters will be located internally in a geometric shape. Shapes such as circles, triangles, and pentagons are considered sacred and are based on ancient philosophies. These shapes may be used to create an internal grid where fragments are housed. Training grids may be simplistic, such as cubes with patterns on them or rows of boxes. More complex grids feature helixes and infinity loops. Greek columns are often associated with time travel programming, and a portal may be located between two columns.

The goal of mind control programming is to subvert the will of the individual. Computers have no will, and they readily accept programming. Highly complex systems with alters and fragments may be contained within what is called a "computer."

Svali writes:

> *"The purpose of the programming in the group that I was in was to organize memories into files and compartments internally, and for these areas to be assigned security levels. This computer is part of the presentation programming, and does not run the*

Programming Themes and Internal Structures

cult host in the larger occultic societies; instead, the host can go internally, flip through the files, and find information they want. But it does assign security levels to memories for the presenters (parts that live their lives in various countries), to prevent them from accidentally accessing memories they are not intended to. My internal computer was put in at MI6 when I was very young; but the template was created earlier by hooking me up to a model of a computer, playing a computerized voice, etc., and convincing the part that they were a computer."

Gems, balls, and multifaceted crystals enhance occult powers in spiritual systems. Mirrors are used internally to reinforce programming sequences such as twinning. They are also used to distort reality and assist in demonic programming. Carousels are used to confuse and punish alters that are told they will be spun on the carousel if they tell what they have experienced. Playing cards are used to reinforce programming by associating certain cards with desired behaviors. Dominoes represent the threat that if the subject tries to undo their programming, a cascade of suicide and other destructive programs will be triggered. Dominoes, dice, and playing cards may be used as codes that grant trainers access to modify a subject's programming. Black boxes, bombs, mines, and booby traps contain self-destruct programming and should not be opened without careful preparation. Spiders and their webs represent demonic programming or programs that link alters or systems. Crystals, clocks, hourglasses, compasses, and many other items are used to introduce or reinforce programming. As you assist a survivor, you might ask them about these objects. If an alter confirms their existence, that information can be used to help deprogram them. Mind control practitioners have found ways to internalize the task of training. Alters are created that perform the tasks of programmers. In some cases, an internal trainer is created that is a replica of an external trainer. Internal training rooms exist that mimic the external training rooms a subject has visited.

Internal walls serve as amnesia barriers. Svali writes:

"A typical use for a wall will be to maintain high levels of amnesia between 'front' or daily living, amnesic alters, and 'back' or cult active alters that contain more of the person's life history. The

EMOTIONAL HEALING AND DELIVERANCE MADE SIMPLE

back may be able to selectively see over and cross past the wall, but the front will be completely unaware that there is a wall, or what lays behind it."

According to Svali, these structures are placed within the subject with the aid of drugs, hypnosis, and electroshock.

"The person is traumatized into a deep trance state. In the deep trance, they will be told to open their eyes and look at either a projected image of the structure, a 3D model of it, or a holographic image using a virtual reality headset. The image will be ground in, using shock and bringing the image closer and closer to the person's visual field. It may be rotated if graphics are available or a 3D is used. They may be told that they are entering inside it, if it is a temple or pyramid, under deep hypnosis, or that they will now live inside the structure, box, card, etc."

❖ Suggestions for Helping Survivors ❖

Svali offers the following suggestions:

"It is important to have good internal communication with both internal alters and an outside therapist while working on color programming. If an individual finds that certain parts believe that they are a certain color, or if this comes up in therapy, they will want to find out if possible how they came to have this belief system. Slowly discovering how the colors were put in will help. Grieving for the vast amount of deception, the amount of abuse heaped on the child, and the very young alters who were the original templates may occur. These parts may be barely verbal, and may want to draw their experiences, or use colors in collages (with the help of older parts inside), to describe to a safe outside person what their reality has been. Validating to them that they are not just a color, that they are part of a whole person, may help.

The survivor may see colored overlays for a while, as they are undoing this programming, as parts inside share their memories. This is normal, although it may feel uncomfortable to see objects as yellow or green, for example. Grounding oneself, having cognitive alters do reality orientation, and patience will help the survivor work through this time.

Jewel programming and metals may be more complex, since the child's sense of uniqueness, pride and status may be bound up in these alters. Rubies, emeralds and diamonds are considered 'high alters' inside and are used to leadership roles, both internally and externally. Acknowledging their importance to the system; listening to them grieve at leaving the cult, which meant giving up their status externally, and giving them new positions inside that are important can help. They can become system leaders in helping the person stay safe, once they make the decision to leave the cult, and become strong allies. But they will often be among the most resistant, and even hostile, to the idea of leaving the cult at first, since they have only known and remembered being rewarded for jobs well done, and have learned to 'pass down' the traumas to 'lower parts' inside. They will often honestly not believe they have been abused, and will only remember being petted or allowed to lead, or being told they were special or valued. Listening to how they feel; acknowledging that leaving means giving up things that were important to them, finding out what needs motivated them, and trying to find healthy outlets for them to get their needs met outside of cult meetings will help. Letting a jewel have leadership within, or chair internal meetings may make up for loss of external leadership when the survivor leaves the cult.

Acknowledging their importance to the survivor is also important. Recognize that these parts are extremely dissociated from their own abuse and trauma, and are in no hurry to remember. But both the survivor and a good therapist can bring reality gently to them, as they let them know that they were abused; that they are actually part of the 'lower emotional parts' who were abused, and will eventually need to acknowledge this. This task takes time and good outside support to accomplish. Allow them to vent their feelings. They will often be highly cognitive at first, but feelings will come, especially grieving, then pain at having been deceived by the cult, then the anguish of realizing that the abuse they passed down to others inside was actually happening to them. They may become quite depressed at this stage, but will also lend tremendous stability and strength to the system, in staying safe and cult free, once they have reached this stage."

CHAPTER THIRTY

Brain Wave Programming

WARNING: SENSITIVE CONTENT — *This chapter contains graphic descriptions of ritual abuse. If you are sensitive or you are a survivor of abuse, you may be triggered and have thoughts of self-harm. Please consider avoiding chapters with this warning, or read them with someone who can provide immediate help.*

THE HUMAN BRAIN OPERATES IN different functional cognitive states that correspond with frequencies that can be detected on an electroencephalogram (EEG). The list below describes the activity of these states along with the corresponding frequency and Greek letter assigned to that brain wave state.

Gamma (35 Hz) Concentration
Beta (12–35 Hz) Anxiety dominant, active, external attention, relaxed
Alpha (8–12 Hz) Very relaxed, passive attention

Theta (4–8 Hz) Deeply relaxed, inward-focused
Delta (0.5–4 Hz) Sleep

The goal of brain wave programming is to create an individual who will accomplish a given task when instructed to. Some jobs are easier to accomplish when the subject is in a particular brain wave state. Alters are created that will automatically take the body into a brain wave state that facilitates completing the needed task. Svali notes that not all cult members are programmed to reach certain brain wave states. The use of this technique varies from region to region. If a child is to undergo the programming, it usually begins when they are around eight years old.

If, for example, a child is to be programmed to reach the delta wave state, their EEG is monitored, and they're given hypnotic drugs. One trainer observes the EEG while another brings the subject into a trance state. Since a system of alters is usually desired that will operate in this brain wave pattern, a template alter is created, usually by splitting one from the core persona. The core spit (or an alter made from it) will become the template from which other alters are formed. The trainer will call up the core split alter and tell them what is expected during the exercise. They will be told to seek a special state called "delta."

The trainer will repeatedly say that delta is good. They will tell the child to perform certain mental exercises, such as counting backward, which helps them reach a deeper trance state. When the trainer monitoring the EEG sees delta waveforms, they will notify the other trainer, who will reward the child. The second trainer will caress the subject, let them know they are in delta, and tell them they're doing well. If the child comes out of the delta state, the trainer will become harsh and shock them as punishment. They will be told they left delta, which is good, and they need to go back into it.

Svali writes:

> *"The induction and counting will be repeated until delta state is seen again, when the child is repeatedly rewarded for entering, then staying in this state for longer and longer periods. The trainers use biofeedback principles to teach the child to consistently cue into a brainwave pattern. When the template alter can stay in the*

Brain Wave Programming

delta pattern consistently, they will be rewarded. This will occur over several months.

The trainers will now have a template that always stays in the delta state that they can begin splitting and using as the basis for forming a new system inside. They will do this using the tools of drugs, hypnosis, and trauma. The new system created will record delta waves on an EEG if done correctly. The new system will be taught what delta means. The trainers will often flash a cue or delta (triangle) symbol on a projector overhead and 'grind in' the delta imprinting. They will wear robes with delta signs on them and clothe the subject in clothing or robes imprinted with the delta sign. They will teach the alters under hypnosis what deltas do and how they act. They will reward them when they comply and shock or otherwise traumatize them if they do not act like 'deltas.' They will be given delta jobs. They will watch high-frequency films that show delta functions. They may build in a computer-like structure to hold the system, showing pictures of its organization while the subject is under deep trance, after creating a clean slate through trauma."

Using this process, alters can be created to access other brain wave states. Each state lends itself to particular tasks. Svali says that alpha is the most easily reached brain wave state. Alters and fragments in this system perform specific asks when activated by triggers such as letters, numbers, phrases, or colors. Sexual alters may be placed in an alpha system. Alters in a beta system tend to be aggressive and will function as cult protectors, internal warriors, and soldiers. A gamma system is home to alters that are highly emotional and extremely loyal to the cult. Suicide alters will be created in this system. Delta alters tend to be cognitive and emotionless. They often have photographic memories and may hold most of the cognitive memories for other systems.

Svali writes:

"Internal programmers, self-destruct, psychotic, and shatter programming as well as other punishment programming sequences to prevent outside access or internal access to the systems may be held within delta systems."

EMOTIONAL HEALING AND DELIVERANCE MADE SIMPLE

Theta systems have alters that participate in blood rituals, sacrifices, and ceremonies. Internal witches, warlocks, seers, psychics, readers, and occult practitioners will be placed in this system.

CHAPTER THIRTY-ONE

Near Death, Assassin, and CIA Programming

WARNING: SENSITIVE CONTENT — *This chapter contains graphic descriptions of ritual abuse. If you are sensitive or you are a survivor of abuse, you may be triggered and have thoughts of self-harm. Please consider avoiding chapters with this warning, or read them with someone who can provide immediate help.*

THE ILLUMINATI WILL USE ANY means necessary to develop loyalty among members. The earlier that devotion to the cult is programmed into a member, the more likely they are to remain loyal over a lifetime. Near-death programming is one way to achieve that goal, and it is done on very young children.

Svali explains that in near-death programming, a toddler will be traumatized during an occult ceremony. They will be beaten, shocked, or suffocated and given drugs to bring them to the brink of death. The

EMOTIONAL HEALING AND DELIVERANCE MADE SIMPLE

child will usually have an out-of-body experience where they view their limp, traumatized body on the verge of death. The child will have their core personality called out, and they'll be given a choice to accept death or choose life, but only if they agree to invite a demon inside.

If the child chooses life, the demon will enter them, and the child usually becomes unconscious. They awaken in a soft bed and find themselves wearing clean clothing. They're told by a kind, soft-voiced person that they died, but the demon brought them back to life, and they owe their life to it and the ones who saved them. The child will be warned that if they ask the demon to leave, they will revert back to the near-death state. This is just one example of how a child may be programmed by a near death experience. Variations on this theme are many, but the goal is the same. The individual is made to believe they are dying and forced to accept help from another cult member or a demon, which requires an oath of lifelong loyalty.

Alters can be programmed to carry out virtually any action, including murder. This appears to have been one of the goals of CIA mind control programs like MK ULTRA that were developed in the middle of the 20th century and investigated by the U.S. Senate. Svali confirms that such programming is commonplace in the Illuminati. The risk in this kind of endeavor is that the programmer could be killed by the subject being programmed. For that reason, the first programming routine installed in a subject is the command to halt whatever they are doing.

Svali writes:

> "When I was a trainer in the Illuminati, there was one command that every trainer learned first when working with their subjects (and assassin training was then mandatory for all children. I went through it, and do not know of any children in the Illuminati who have not). The command? The 'halt' command. This is the first command put in. It freezes the child, teen, or adult in place and it is ground in.
>
> Why do trainers learn this code first for the person they work with? Because of the real risk that the person may try to kill them and the halt code bypasses this."

Near Death, Assassin, and CIA Programming

Svali continues:

> "At night, I knew trainers (who were sloppy or pushed too hard) who were killed by the person they were working on. It was considered one of the risks of the job. I was always cautious. All trainers knew that at night, a person might get out of control. The person was highly punished for it, locked up for days, tortured to teach them that it wasn't okay. If the person became very unstable, they might be considered 'expendable' and eliminated. Or sent to a state hospital, where no one would believe their 'paranoid fantasies' of being taught to assassinate others."

The 12 steps of discipline mentioned previously include programming cult members to fire weapons. Initially, they train with air guns. Later they learn to shoot rifles and pistols and practice their techniques using virtual reality equipment.

Svali says:

> "Members are trained to kill coldly and emotionlessly on command and to shoot their brother or sister during virtual reality exercises, and they believe it is real under hypnotic trance, to test their obedience. (They actually did this horrible thing to my son, and he cried as he told how anxious he was the next day, and almost died of shock to see his sister alive and well. That was the only way he knew it had been a virtual reality exercise and not real)."

After being tortured over a period of years, members are programmed to direct their anger at their targets and become better marksmen.

Svali writes:

> "People do not suddenly become killers. It is a learned process to overcome the natural horror of killing other human beings, a process begun in earliest childhood by the Illuminati. You have to force a child to kill. Here is how it is done (how it was done to me):
>
> 1. When the child is two years old, place them in a metal cage with electrodes attached. Shock the child severely.

EMOTIONAL HEALING AND DELIVERANCE MADE SIMPLE

2. Take the child out, and place a kitten in its hands. Tell the child to wring the kitten's neck. The child will cry and refuse.

3. Put the child into the cage, and shock them until they are dazed and cannot scream anymore.

4. Take the child out, and tell them again to wring the kitten's neck. This time the child will shake all over and cry, but do it because they are afraid of torture. The child will then go into the corner and vomit while the adult praises them for 'doing such a good job.'

This is the first step. The animals get bigger over time as the child gets older. They will be forced to kill an infant at some point, either in reality, a setup (staged event), or virtual reality. They will be taught by age nine to put together a gun, to aim, and fire on target and on command. They will then practice on realistic manikins. They will then practice on animals. They will then practice on 'expendables' or in virtual reality. They will be highly praised if they do well and tortured if they don't comply.

The older the child or teen, the more advanced the training. By age 15, most children will also be forced to do hand-to-hand combat in front of spectators (high people who come to watch the 'games' much as the ancient gladiators performed). These matches are rarely done to the death, usually until one child goes down. They use every type of weapon imaginable and learn to fight for their lives. If a child loses a fight, they are heavily punished by their trainer, who loses face. If they win, they are again praised for being strong and adept with weapons. By the time they are 21, they are well-trained combat/killing machines with command codes to kill, and they have been tested over and over to prove that they will obey on command. This is how children in the German Illuminati are brought up. I went through it myself."

Alleged Central Intelligence Programming

Svali claims members of the Illuminati serve as operatives for intelligence agencies. Programming can include creating alters that are able

Near Death, Assassin, and CIA Programming

to locate a target, study them while avoiding detection, and seduce or assassinate them. The average human only uses a fraction of their mental capacity. The Illuminati understand this, and according to Svali, they've developed a way to utilize more of the brain. By placing subjects in a trance state, photographic memory is developed.

Svali writes:

> "A person under hypnosis will have almost complete recall of events and details around them. The brain never loses anything. It is just that in daily life, we filter out information to allow normal function. Otherwise, our senses would be bombarded, and we would be constantly distracted. Alters may be trained to become hyper-aware of their environment and able to overhear conversations that are whispered. Internal recording alters are taught to download these conversations, as well as other information. Photographic recall is emphasized, as the person will be hypnotized or put into a delta state for 'downloading' information to the trainer or CIA operative."

A child that is being programmed will attend a dinner party or other role-playing exercise set up by the trainer.

Svali writes:

> "There will be a group, anywhere from ten to sixteen people at the party. Afterward, the child will be questioned by the trainer extensively. Who was sitting where? What were they wearing? What color were their eyes? Their hair? Who gave the speech? What did they say? The child will be praised for correct answers but punished and shocked if they're unable to recall details. This is to reinforce natural photographic memory and assist the child with recording details. The next few times, the child's abilities will improve, as they want to avoid punishment."

Svali continues:

> "In the next level of training, the child will be asked to observe and figure out: who is the most important person in the room?

EMOTIONAL HEALING AND DELIVERANCE MADE SIMPLE

Why? They will be taught body movements, and mannerisms, that give nonverbal clues away. The child may be taught to approach important adults, or an assigned target, first in role-play, later in real life, and engage them in innocuous conversation while looking for information they have been clued to get. They may be taught to be innocently seductive and will be dressed for the part. They will frequently be taught to lure the target into having intercourse with them.

An older youth or adult will be taught not only how to lure a target into bed but later how to kill them if they are an assassination target, while they are asleep or relaxing after sexual relations. They will be taught to go through the target's belongings for any information needed by the trainer or cult leader. Often, before an assignment for an assassination, the cult member will be indoctrinated with reasons why killing the victim is a service to humanity. They will be lied to and told that they are the head of a pornography ring, a pedophile, or a brutal villain. This will engage the assassin's natural anger towards the person and will motivate them while helping to overcome their natural moral reluctance and guilt at killing a human being.

They will be taught how to disguise themselves with a change of clothing, sex (masquerading as the opposite sex), makeup, contact lenses, and getting out of the situation safely. They will be taught how to overcome interrogation techniques with extensive training and hypnosis in case they are ever caught. They will be taught to self-suicide with a pill or dagger if they are ever apprehended."

❖ Suggestions for Helping Survivors ❖

Svali offers the following suggestions for assisting those who have been programmed using these methods:

"CIA programming will involve the use of sophisticated technology to reinforce its effectiveness and can be difficult to break. It may involve the person being traumatized in isolation tanks (this will also be done with brain wave programming). It may involve sensory

deprivation, sensory overload, isolation, and sleep deprivation. It may involve hours of listening to repetitive tapes on headphones. The subject is shocked or severely punished if they try to remove the headphones. They will be hypnotized, tortured, subjected to different drug combinations, and exposed to harmonic tones, often in one ear or the other. They will be exposed to flashing strobe lights, which may induce a seizure, and alters will be programmed to cause seizures if the subject tries to break their programming. They will be shown high-speed films with different tracks, one for the left eye and one for the right eye, to increase brain splitting or dichotomous thinking.

The survivor and therapist need to work slowly to undo the effects of this trauma. The person will need to come to terms, slowly and carefully, with how the programming was done. They may need to learn their own access codes (this will also be true of brain wave and other sophisticated programming techniques). They will need to communicate with the traumatized alters and fragments to let them know they were used. They will need to help the young alters, who were split to create the system and often underwent the worst traumas. Grieving for the abuse, the trauma, the methodical calculation used and scientific methods used to put in this programming will take time. Venting feelings, including rage, and safely will be important. The survivor may be afraid of strong feelings and will fear, especially anger and rage, since they will associate those feelings with having to kill, hurt, or assassinate others. Allowing the feelings to be expressed slowly and carefully, being aware that homicidal and suicidal feelings will probably come up, is important.

If there is a concern about the ability to control acting out, the client may need to go as an inpatient to a safe facility that understands mind control and cult programming. They will fear being labeled 'psychotic' since the programmers told them that they would be called this and locked up forever. The worst thing a therapist or hospital can do in a situation like this is play into those fears or label the person psychotic. Constant grounding in reality, using grounding exercises, slow, careful venting of rage and betrayal feelings, reinforcing over and over that the survivor can remember and not go psychotic, or die, believing and validating the survivor are all important. The survivor may have unstable behavior at points, but this is not psychosis, but rather, the natural reaction to extreme trauma. The survivor needs to realize this and that they can overcome its effects with time and good therapy. They will need hope and a good support system."

CHAPTER THIRTY-TWO

Types of Alters and Fragments

> **WARNING: SENSITIVE CONTENT** — *This chapter contains graphic descriptions of ritual abuse. If you are sensitive or you are a survivor of abuse, you may be triggered and have thoughts of self-harm. Please consider avoiding chapters with this warning, or read them with someone who can provide immediate help.*

THOSE WHO ARE SUBJECTED TO mind control and ritual abuse have a diversity of alters and fragments within them, which serve unique purposes. This chapter describes some of the more common ones.

Protector alters are created to preserve the life of the individual who experiences abuse. They tend to be formidable, aggressive, unemotional, and untrusting. Protector alters can interfere with personal relationships. But, in the healing process, they can be recruited to protect the survivor from further abuse.

EMOTIONAL HEALING AND DELIVERANCE MADE SIMPLE

Cults need intellectual alters who can observe events, assimilate information, commit it to memory, and transfer it to outsiders. Intellectual alters pass information between systems. These alters might be recorders, computers, or scholars. They may know several languages, have a scientific inclination, or be versed in different philosophies. Brilliant and cognitive, they often believe that they can outwit those around them, including therapists. But they also know much of the survivor's life history that the others don't. These parts can recite the life history of the individual without emotion. For this reason, intellectual alters can be used to provide information about how the survivor was programmed, which can aid in deprogramming. When they are out, the individual will have a flat affect.

A subtype of intellectual alter is the denial alter. Their task is to deny that the survivor was abused. Because other types of alters carry emotions, they are disconnected from the pain of trauma and find it easy to deny that it happened. They are programmed to believe that the survivor's life has been wonderful, their parents loving, and their upbringing perfectly normal. They fear they may suffer punishment if the survivor remembers the abuse.

A controller is a leader in a system of alters. They have a broad awareness of what is happening in their system at all times. In a military system, such a controller alter may have the rank of General. In a protector system, they will be the most powerful protector. In a metals system, they will be the highest-ranking metal such as gold or platinum. In a jewel system, they will be the highest-ranking jewel, such as a diamond or emerald.

Svali writes:

> *"Usually, there are several leaders in a system that share the responsibility. They can also become invaluable helpers over time if they choose to give up cult loyalty."*

Child alters (sometimes called "littles") desire praise from the adults and leaders in their system and may come out for a reward, such as candy. Out of fear and the hope of being rewarded, they will report on other alters until they are taught that it is safe not to do so. They

Types of Alters and Fragments

are often the heart of a system and can feel love, joy, and fear. When they are out, they like being hugged and being told that they are okay.

When punishment is severe and frequent, survivors will create an internal alter that mimics the perpetrator in an attempt to keep themselves in line and avoid physical punishment. (An alter that resembles an individual outside the system is called an introject.)

Svali notes:

> "The cult will capitalize on this, and often trainers will leave as their 'calling card'— an alter named after themselves. This one will be an internal trainer, punisher, or enforcer. Their job is to keep things in line, and they will often try to sabotage therapy. They are often fearful of external punishment if they don't do their job. Internal punishers will also activate self-punishment sequences inside (such as flood programming, suicide programming, or other self-harm sequences) if the person begins breaking away from the cult and the old rules. These parts may take time to convince that they can change their old way of doing things since they were often accountable to the outside handler/trainer if things weren't kept in line."

The young survivor of ritual abuse is routinely overwhelmed by emotions such as pain and despair. When one's survival is threatened, they may resort to creating alters or fragments that hold onto painful emotions. Dividing the emotions among a group of alters and fragments can make the situation more manageable. Feeling alters are often isolated from the rest of the system to minimize their effect on others.

Svali writes:

> "When they come out in therapy, the feeling may hit 'full force' at first. A child alter may come out screaming, terror-stricken, or wailing in uncontrollable grief and pain until they are grounded in the here and now. Often, feelings were heavily punished in the cult, so it was psychologically necessary to bury them deeply within the psyche in order to survive. These parts may be very separated from the parts that know what happened to cause the feelings in

a highly fragmented system, so that the feelings seem to come out of nowhere, without any cause. With time and healing, they can hook up with the intellectuals inside who observed, and other parts who went through the same trauma, giving meaning to the feelings and helping to resolve them."

Most cults have leadership councils, and many survivors internalize them. It's another way survivors are taught to internalize perpetrators.

Svali writes:

"A person may have a local leadership council internalized, or spiritual councils that represent outside people, such as an internal druidic council or group of ascended masters that help run things inside."

When alters understand that they are no longer needed as overseers, they can be re-tasked with helping other alters see their need for healing.

Sexual alters are created to offload the trauma of childhood sexual abuse. They hold onto the emotions and cognitive ideas that a young child cannot handle. Some sexual alters are trained to enjoy the abuse (or pretend to) and are heavily rewarded.

Amnesic alters are tasked with forgetting the survivor's abuse. They are often found in the front system and manage day-to-day affairs. As a child, they were punished if they remembered. Although they are content to have no memory of abuse, the parts that know about the abuse may envy or dislike them. This may lead to internal battles between systems. Amnesic parts must slowly accept that the abuse did happen. Reminding other parts that the amnesia saved the child's (and their) life may be helpful. A survivor may have an alter (or system) that serves as a daytime host and a different alter for nighttime. Many times, a unique host (or system) will be developed to handle special events and rituals.

Svali writes:

"Function codes, access codes, halt codes, and system codes are fragments that might be put into a system to do certain jobs and

are created to only do that job when called out by triggers such as letters, numbers, phrases, or other auditory stimuli. These are created with deep trauma and are very intentionally done by perpetrators.

Spiritual parts: these may have a variety of beliefs that cover different spiritualities internally. There may be one overriding spiritual belief for the system or several. For example, a spiritual system created by the cult may include aspects of Luciferianism, druidism, Temple of Set teachings, Ancient Babylonian mystery religions, etc. The host or presenters may have a completely conflicting religious belief system, and there may be hostility between the parts that hold opposing beliefs. In my own life, my presenters were strong Christians, and this gave me the stability and comfort needed to bring healing to the parts inside. It also opened the way to begin forgiveness, one of the most difficult and important tasks in the healing process."

CHAPTER THIRTY-THREE

Healing the Survivor

I KNOW MANY SURVIVORS OF trauma-based mind control. I first suspect someone may be a survivor by the behavioral changes exhibited when alters switch. If you spend any amount of time around a survivor, you'll notice dramatic mood changes, different mannerisms, sudden changes of topic in conversations, and significant periods of amnesia. Most survivors have a history of repeated suicide attempts, with or without a diagnosis of depression. All of these are clues that a person is a survivor of ritual abuse. If you suspect that someone you know is a survivor, you might ask them if they would like to discuss the matter. If they agree, and if it seems they are indeed a survivor, you might offer to assist them in healing and deprogramming.

Svali has good recommendations for deprogramming and healing survivors of mind control. However, most readers are not qualified to offer psychiatric services such as therapy. I would add to her suggestions the principles of Christ-centered emotional healing. It has been my experience, and that of others who work in the healing community, that Jesus can heal and integrate even the most complex system of alters. When a complex system is involved, it will take time and patience. Steve Harmon has kept me updated on his work of freeing a survivor named Mercy, who suffered severe ritual abuse. Her systems were incredibly complex and riddled with traps. It took more than five years to gain victory over her programming. Her story is a testimony to the fact that a patient, Christ-centered approach to healing complex trauma can be effective.

Cults see their members as prized possessions and will stop at nothing to get them back once they leave. Svali tells of how she was allowed supervised visits with her children for several years after leaving the Illuminati. She thought it odd that she had not been re-accessed by the cult. Years later, in therapy, it was revealed that she had been re-accessed repeatedly during her visits with her children. Alters that were loyal to the cult hid from her the fact that she was being reprogrammed by the cult during each visit. If you leave a cult and experience no signs of being re-accessed, that should raise a red flag and make you consider if perhaps you're not seeing the whole picture.

Programmers use grids and maps to give them an overview of a survivor's systems. If you endeavor to deprogram someone, you should create at least a basic map or list of the individual's systems. Control alters should be questioned, and the information gleaned from them should be used to create a map or list. On the theme of safety, higher functioning alters should be asked about internal traps, black boxes, and suicide or other self-destruct codes. Information provided should be used to carefully undo this programming.

Alters and fragments—even ones that act primarily in destructive ways—often have good and noble intentions. But their perspective is heavily influenced by the pain they experience and by demonic programming. The reality of suffering is many times worse for a fragment who may be suspended in a traumatic memory where they continually experience abuse. They simply want the pain to end. A demon may suggest that suicide is the solution. An alter or fragment may believe that if they were allowed to carry out a plan of suicide, it would be better for the

Healing the Survivor

individual because the pain would end. They mean well, but their view of what is best for the individual is distorted. They don't understand that suicide means the death of themselves, the entire system, and the physical body. (Some alters reject the notion that the physical body is theirs. Thus, they don't see the death of the body as a problem.) Demons reinforce the programmed beliefs that pain will be eternal, that no one can be trusted, that the alter must remain in control and that suicide is the solution.

The safety of the survivor must be the top priority. Helping those who are entertaining thoughts of suicide is risky. If the individual is making active threats or gestures of suicide, the safest plan is to assist them in getting help from a mental health professional. Typically, this would include an evaluation either at a hospital or mental health facility. But if the individual is not making active threats or gestures of suicide, it may be safe to help them with emotional healing.

Our goal is healing and deprogramming the alters and fragments caused by trauma-based mind control. Healing is the removal of guilt, shame, rage, pain, or other negative emotions and removing demons. Deprogramming amounts to changing an individual's way of thinking. Cooperative alters are easy to heal, but many alters and fragments are influenced by demons. Demonic influence makes them less cooperative. A demon's goal may be to keep an alter in fear of further abuse. An alter that fears abuse believes it must remain in control to keep the individual safe. Before interacting with an alter, you might consider commanding demons that influence them to be silent. This will decrease demonic interference.

The first step in healing an alter is making contact with them. If someone is not aware they have alters, I usually ask them to recall a traumatic event. I'm attempting to trigger an alter and have them respond to me. Since alters and fragments retain the memories of trauma, asking the individual to recall a traumatic event is one way to make contact. If the person knows they have alters, ask them to list their names (if they are known). Then ask one of the alters to come up. Look for a change in mood, affect, or mannerisms. Another approach to making contact is exploring the person's system in your mind. The Holy Spirit or Jesus can lead you to an alter they want to heal.

EMOTIONAL HEALING AND DELIVERANCE MADE SIMPLE

Once you make contact with an alter, start a conversation with them. Let them know they are loved and appreciated. Ask them what they do for the individual. There are many different roles alters can play and a great diversity of responsibilities they can assume. If an alter describes their function as a protector, for example, tell them you respect them and that you appreciate the help they provide. Affirm them in whatever way is appropriate. An alter that serves as a protector will have a strong sense of duty. They may see themselves as brave and courageous—the only one standing between a vulnerable individual and a world that wants to harm them.

Noble as they are, even the most courageous alters experience feelings of overwhelm and defeat. This can be used as an opening to discuss their role as protector and introduce them to the ultimate protector—Jesus. Explain that Jesus has never been defeated, can always be trusted, and is far more capable of protecting the individual than them. If the alter argues that Jesus doesn't care about them because He did not prevent their abuse, point out that He cannot overrule the free will of humans. Remind them that He was with the person during the abuse, and He never left their side. Ask if they'll allow Jesus to show them where He was during the traumatic event. The main tactic here is encouraging the alter to trust Jesus. If they agree to meet Him, make the introduction. Jesus will usually demonstrate His love for them in some way. He may show them a view of the traumatic event from a perspective they've never seen. This new perspective will destroy the programmed belief that no one can be trusted. Encouragement, instruction, and displays of love create new programming in the minds of alters.

After gaining their trust, ask if they would like Jesus to remove their pain. When they agree, Jesus will heal them. You might ask a healed alter if they'll spread the word to other alters that Jesus can be trusted and that He can heal them. If the alter agrees, and if other alters ask to meet Jesus or express the desire to be healed, facilitate the healing. After an alter is healed, they'll usually be given a choice of going to be with Jesus in heaven or integrating back into the core of the soul. Jesus and the alter usually decide how this will be done.

When child alters come up, they should be shown platonic love and affection. Once their trust is gained, they can be introduced to Jesus, who will heal and integrate them or take them to heaven. Alters and fragments that hold emotions should be allowed to express their emotions when they come up. Offer them an opportunity to allow Jesus to take their pain, heal them, and integrate them when they are ready. Perpetrator alters are likely to resist healing. They're driven by fear of physical punishment for failing to follow programming directives. The goal is to convince them that it is not necessary to keep alters in line for fear of punishment. Making sure the survivor is not re-accessed by the cult will help relieve these fears. Show them love. Gain their trust, and ask them to allow Jesus to take away their fear and pain.

Be aware that cults frequently program alters as false Messiahs. Sometimes, a false Jesus will be a demon. These false Christs are usually abusive to alters. You may meet rejection when asking an alter who has met a sadistic false Christ to meet your Jesus. This is an opportunity to teach them about the difference between a false Christ and the real Jesus. If an alter says they have already met Jesus and they don't trust Him, ask them to describe the Jesus they met. They may describe a portrait they saw of Jesus or a sinister-looking man who punished them. Ask them about the eyes of Jesus. Many people report seeing love in the eyes of the real Jesus and malevolence in the eyes of a false Christ. For many alters, a time of discipleship will be required before they are ready to be healed and integrated. Teaching them the realities of God's love and demonstrating it regularly will facilitate their healing.

I can't provide precise instructions for healing every alter or fragment you will encounter, but I can offer general guidelines. The safety of the survivor comes first. Create a running list or diagram that captures the features of the inner world. Allow alters and fragments to express emotions, grieve, ask questions, and adjust to the reality of their situation. Demonstrations of love and acceptance will help the healing process more than anything. When they are ready, offer alters and fragments an opportunity to meet Jesus. Follow His lead when it comes to their healing and integration.

For a person with many alters, the healing process can be lengthy. Multiple sessions are typically needed. Jesus can provide specific strategies and tactics for each session. Try to identify alters that want to be healed. Certain alters may be willing to receive encouragement or instruction.

Provide support, instruction, and affirmation as needed until an alter or fragment is ready to be healed.

CHAPTER THIRTY-FOUR

Learning to Love

I USED TO LAUGH AT the Israelites for the stubbornness that caused them to spend 40 years wandering in the wilderness. As I neared the end of a 35-year career in medicine, I came to the painful realization that I'm just as hard-hearted as them. The Israelites knew that giants inhabited the promised land and thought it too difficult to overpower them. They disobeyed God and remained in the wilderness. I failed to obey the one thing He has asked of His people—to love others unconditionally.

It isn't difficult to love those who treat us well. But it seems impossible to love those who are cruel to us. The command to love my enemies had been hammered into my head. My brain understood the message perfectly. But it didn't' seem to penetrate the junkyard that had become my soul. And it's there, among the wounds and raw emotions of my past, that the admonition to love others remained powerless.

While working as a paramedic in Tacoma, Washington, I regularly transported an alcoholic who had made a career out of pestering paramedics at the most inconvenient hours. In the middle of the night, we'd go out in search of him. Once we found him, we'd toss him on the gurney and dump him off at the nearest hospital. He'd complain on the way there about how bad the ride was. If he was having a worse-than-normal day, he'd shower us with spit and hurl curses at us. I remember the time he asked my partner to shake his hand. She innocently grasped his hand, and he gripped it with all his strength until she screamed for him to let go. He did cruel things like this every day to those of us who worked in emergency services. He felt a sense of pleasure (or maybe accomplishment) when he inflicted pain on others.

I've counseled people who have suffered abuse and torture at the hands of their relatives. I've heard of things being done to them that are so perverted and sick it makes me wonder how they're still alive. How can we ever come to love such mean, perverted, and heartless people the way Jesus asked us to?

If it were easy, I would have done it long ago. Instead, like most people who work in health care, I've repressed my thoughts of loathing and hatred toward the people I've transported because that's what is expected of me. My employer can make me act professionally toward an abusive patient, but they can't keep me from hating them. And I've spent most of my life silently despising many of the people I've transported. When paramedics and nurses gather in the break room of a hospital, we share our favorite stories about the system abusers we treat. It's how we bond. And perhaps more importantly, it's how we justify our hatred toward them.

Those who abuse us do so because they're emotionally wounded. When someone abuses others as an adult, it's because they've been abused as a child. Abuse is a learned behavior.

A few years ago, after I had seen success with physical healing, I became discontented with not seeing my patients healed of mental illness. One night, I asked God for the key to healing mental illness. That night, He gave me a message in a dream. The message was simple: mental illness is healed through love.

I didn't like that answer. I expected a formula (even though I know He doesn't use them). Consciously, I objected to the idea because it seemed too simple. Subconsciously, I objected it because it seemed too difficult. Loving those who hurt you is a simple idea until you try to do it.

The desire to harm and abuse others germinates and spreads in an environment devoid of love. And if the absence of love is the cause of a malady, the presence of it is certain to be the cure.

When we withhold love from those who are emotionally traumatized—the ones who abuse us out of their own pain—we withhold the only thing that can cure them. If they are ever going to be healed, they need to receive love. And ironically, love is the one thing we are unable to give them.

At this point, I'd like to make clear what I'm *not* saying:

I am not suggesting that we must allow abusive people to continue abusing us. No one deserves to be abused. It's unwise to remain in an abusive relationship if you can leave. I'm also not justifying abusive behavior. Abuse is never an acceptable behavior. I'm only offering a theory of how abuse happens and a way in which it might be cured.

The world is full of broken people who would harm us if they had the chance. It seems unlikely that we can avoid abusive people entirely since in many cases, the behavior we encounter personally doesn't begin until we're committed to a relationship. It seems there are three ways we can respond to abusive people:

One option is to guard ourselves against abusive people and treat them like an enemy. Many people choose to live this way. It forces one to be hyper-vigilant, and mistrusting, and it leads to a life of isolation. A second option is to ignore abusive people and try to keep their behavior from affecting us. A third is to see them the way God sees them: as wounded, hurting children who don't understand what they are doing and don't know how to get free of the cycle of violence they're trapped in.

The only way I've been able to consistently show love and compassion toward someone who makes me want to scream is to picture them, in my mind, as they might have been at the age of three or four. It is easier to extend grace to children when they act inappropriately. We don't hold children to the same behavioral standards that we do adults. And since, in some cases, we're dealing with people who have fragments and alters that are at the developmental age of a child, it might be more appropriate to see them this way.

I'm not suggesting that we treat an abusive person as if they were a child. That will only annoy them. Instead, I'm suggesting that we choose to see them (internally) as if we were seeing a child and extend to them the same grace and patience we would a child. It's an internal response—a choice to love them despite the messes they've made. After all, love is not an emotion. It is a choice to act benevolently toward another, irrespective of how we feel about them.

Steve Harmon has worked for years with severely traumatized people who have been diagnosed with schizophrenia, psychosis, dissociative identity disorder, bipolar and other behavioral problems. He's found that of all the techniques he's used, nothing heals emotionally traumatized people as quickly as loving them unconditionally.

Jesus didn't command us to love others because He wanted us to wrestle with an impossible task. He gave us the command because the power of love sets tortured people free. It frees them, and it frees us.

Loving our abuser is impossible to do in our own strength. But once God's love has enlightened the darkened places of our soul, it becomes easier to extend that same love to those who are cruel to us. The starting point is encountering the radical, life-giving love of God. If you haven't been embraced by the Father's love yet, ask Him to show you in a tangible way how much He loves you.

INKITY PRESS

Other books from Praying Medic
For up-to-date titles go to: PrayingMedic.com

Series—The Kingdom of God Made Simple:
Divine Healing Made Simple
Seeing in the Spirit Made Simple
Hearing God's Voice Made Simple
Traveling in the Spirit Made Simple
Dream Interpretation Made Simple
Power and Authority Made Simple
Emotional Healing Made Simple

Series—My Craziest Adventures with God:
My Craziest Adventures with God - Volume 1
My Craziest Adventures with God - Volume 2

Series—The Courts of Heaven:
Defeating Your Adversary in the Court of Heaven
Operating in the Court of Angels

And more:
Emotional Healing in 3 Easy Steps
The Gates of Shiloh (a novel)
God Speaks: Perspectives on Hearing God's Voice (28 authors)
A Kingdom View of Economic Collapse (eBook only)
American Sniper: Lessons in Spiritual Warfare (eBook only)

SCAN THIS TO GO TO
PrayingMedic.com

Made in the USA
Coppell, TX
10 December 2023